LIFE IN THE WILDERNESS

Reflections on the Exodus and Our Journey to the Promised Land

◊

Don Johnson

Contents

Introduction   7

Chapter 1   New Life and a Narrow Road   **11**

Chapter 2   Sacrifice   **35**

Chapter 3   Testing God   **57**

Chapter 4   The Body and Blood of Christ   **75**

Chapter 5   The Reason for the Rules   **87**

Chapter 6   The Seriousness of Sin   **101**

Chapter 7   The Necessity of Perseverance   **123**

Chapter 8   God With Us   **147**

Chapter 9   The Comfort Trap   **163**

Chapter 10   The Trustworthiness of God   **181**

Notes   **193**

Introduction

Homesick for Heaven

I have a great life. My wife is a smart, talented and gracious woman who loves me even though I lack all of those qualities. My kids are a blast; being a dad to them brings me great joy. Even going to work is fun for me, as I find my career incredibly interesting and rewarding. On top of all that, I have great friends and a nice place to live. There is no doubt that I am incredibly blessed.

Yet in spite of all the good, I am not completely satisfied. There are still too many problems in each day and too much sorrow in the midst of the joy. Even as awesome as my life is, I can't shake the sense that it isn't all that it should be. I want something more.

My situation is not unique, of course. A simple fact of existence is that people are not content. Even in the affluent West, with the highest standard of living in the history of the world, pollsters tell us that people are not truly and deeply happy.[1] No matter how much we have, we all want something more.

For some, this never-ending attempt to fill a void can lead to despair. Think of the long list of celebrities who have reached the top of their profession (and society's ladder) only to fall into depression and destructive behavior over the lack of fulfillment they find there.

For others, it simply means, as Thoreau said, a life of quiet desperation. They work and play and watch some TV and try to not think too much about the void inside.

Thankfully, I have learned that I do not have to succumb to either of those options because there is a good explanation for my unfulfilled condition and plenty of good reasons to believe that it will not last forever.

The Answer

The reason nothing on Earth satisfies my innermost longings is that I do not actually long for anything on Earth. As C.S. Lewis reasoned,[2] "If I find in myself a desire which no experience in this world can satisfy, the most probable explanation is that I was made for another world."[3]

That other world is Heaven.[4] Heaven is what I am missing, what I am longing for. My deepest problem on Earth is that I do not belong here. I was created to live in the presence of God and existing anywhere else will leave me unfulfilled. This is true for everyone. In the words of Randy Alcorn, we are homesick.

> Nothing is more often misdiagnosed than our homesickness for Heaven. We think that what we want is sex, drugs, alcohol, a new job, a raise, a doctorate, a spouse, a large-screen television, a new car, a cabin in the woods, a condo in Hawaii. What we really want is the person we were made for, Jesus, and the place we were made for, Heaven. Nothing less can satisfy us.[5]

Ultimately, I am frustrated because I live on a fallen planet. When Adam and Even sinned, they were expelled from their natural home and exiled from God. Everyone born into the world since that time has the same problem: we aren't where we are supposed to be.

This book is about the solution; the journey to where we belong. In the pages that follow, I discuss a few different aspects of that trip and offer some scriptural principles for accomplishing it successfully.

These principles are based on the example of the Israelites and the Exodus. Several years ago, I started studying the book of Exodus in order to teach a class at my church. It was a life changing experience. Although I had known the basic story all m y life, that study caused me to see it with new eyes. A whole new theological vista opened for me as I realized just how much typological truth is contained in the Exodus story. By that I mean that I began to understand how many aspects of the narrative are meant to show us specific truths about ourselves, God, and his plan for our redemption. From the Exodus story we can learn not just how God acted in the ancient past, but how he is working today and how he plans to operate in the future. The Israelite's story is our story, and it is the story of our children.

Take, as an example, the Israelites as slaves in Egypt. They were separated from their true home and powerless to do anything about it. As such, their situation is a perfect allegorical picture of the human condition since the fall: Egypt is Earth, the Egyptian ruler, Pharaoh, is Satan and the Promised Land, Canaan, is Heaven. Just like the Israelites, we find ourselves living under a tyrannical ruler in a foreign land without the power to do anything about it. Taking it further (which we will do in greater detail throughout this book), in the same way that God rescued the Israelites, he rescues us. The historical account of the Israelites is not just a picture of living in slavery to a foreign tyrant. It also describes salvation from that situation, both for them and for us. The extraordinary tale of the Israelites' escape from slavery and journey to the Promised Land is a metaphorical roadmap of the path to Heaven. The story of their redemption is meant to instruct us about what is necessary for ours. By learning how the Israelites arrived (or failed to arrive) at their home, we can learn how to reach our own Promised Land.

Realizations such as this enriched my understanding of God's plan for the world, altered my view of salvation, and deepened my relationship with God. Since that time I have continued to study the Exodus story, continually finding new and exciting truths. It has become an integral part of my life and my ministry. Interestingly, the more I learn, the more it seems like I am still just scratching the surface. With that caveat, then, I offer some reflections[6] on the Israelite's journey to the Promised Land. I pray that they will be as helpful to you as they have been to me.

Chapter 1

New Life and a Narrow Road

Thinking like a Child

I clearly remember the moment I became a Christian. I don't recall how old I was exactly, probably six or seven, but it was a Sunday afternoon and I had been to church that morning. Something about Sunday School must have made an impression on me, because I asked my mother to come to my room to talk to me about getting saved. She graciously led me in a prayer of repentance and faith and as we finished, I felt great joy and relief sweep over me and I knew that I was going to get into Heaven.

If you had asked me at the time what it meant to be "saved" I'm not sure what I would have told you. However, as I think back now to the theology of my youth, several images come to mind.

For one, I considered salvation as a type of fire insurance. To avoid hell, make sure you sign on the dotted line by doing whatever the preacher says you need to do ("believe," "repent," "have faith," "give your life to Jesus," etc.) and then rest easy, knowing that you are covered. Your papers are in order and when that fateful day arrives, everything will be just fine.

Along the same lines, I thought that "getting saved" was like making a reservation at a very ritzy and exclusive club. As long as you had made that phone call at some point in your life, when you show up at the pearly gates, St. Peter will see that your name is in the book and welcome you in!

In more familial and relational terms, I thought of becoming a child of God as a one time legal transaction in which I got a new guardian. In my mind, joining

God's family was a bit like being adopted by a rich foreign benefactor with whom I didn't get to see or live. To flesh that out a bit, I thought of humanity as a bunch of street urchins living in a slum. One day God drives up in a fancy limousine and gets those of us that are willing to sign some papers acknowledging that we want to be in his family. He then registers our name and calls us his. Before leaving again, he gives us a new coat to wear with his insignia on it, vowing one day to return (in an even fancier car) to take us home with him to live with him in a mansion. When that finally happens, we will get all the rest of the benefits of being his children: our own spacious bedroom, private school, all the gourmet food we can eat, etc. In the meantime, we can relax in the fact that we have a new name and a new coat and that God does not view us as dirty urchins anymore, but rather as his children. He sees the jacket that we wear, not the wretched mess that is inside it.

This whole arrangement seemed to me a bit like a professional sports player moving from one franchise to another. The person stays the same but the jersey he wears is different. Joe the Football Star is still the same Joe on the inside, even if he looks different on the outside come game-day. Interestingly, for fans, the externals are usually all that matters. Those people that hated Joe when he played for the archrival will now cheer their hearts out for him when he takes to the field for the home team. Fans don't look on the inside, they only see the outside. That is how I thought God worked. He wasn't that concerned with what was actually going on inside a person; he looked only on the exterior, and thankfully he had signed me to be on his team.

I make this doctrinal confession in order to help explain why, for many years, I lived such a spiritually pathetic life. By that I mean that, among other things, I was enslaved to the same sins that plague the unsaved and I operated according to the same worldly priorities as they do, all the while remaining confident of my own salvation.

This is not to say that I just sinned rampantly and accepted every evil the world offered. I tried to live a reasonably good life in appreciation for what God had done for me. (And if I remember correctly, that was usually the reason given by pastors to motivate us to moral behavior.) But I didn't pursue a life of radical righteousness or intimacy with God, largely because I didn't think it was possible or consider it something God was all that interested in. Basically, I lived by the bumper sticker adage "I'm not perfect, just forgiven." The point of that sticker, it seems to me, is that being forgiven is the important thing, not trying to be perfect.

This was consistent with my theology. I don't remember ever being taught this explicitly, but the practical consequence of my view of salvation at the time is that "Children of God" or "Christians" can stay essentially unchanged on the inside. That is exactly what I did, because I didn't think it mattered to God what my insides looked like anyway. He didn't take that into consideration. Rather, he chose to look only on the outside, and he had painted my outside with a "Jesus covering." God didn't see my sin and worldly ambition; he only saw the covering he had placed on me. I figured that I may not be actually righteous, but God saw me as legally righteous, so everything was alright.

More than a One Time Legal Transaction

I now understand that I was wrong, or at least insufficiently right. Certainly there is a legal element to entering into God's family and some aspects of my old model can find biblical support, including in the Exodus account. In fact, later in the book we will discuss the legal aspects of redemption when we talk about how

Christ is the Lamb of God and what it means to get covered by his blood. Also, I acknowledge that becoming "adopted" by God in this manner would absolutely be better than having God do nothing. Being given a jacket and taken to a mansion later is better than being left for all time in the slum. However, the problem is in what I was missing. My understanding simply didn't take into account all that God actually does and thereby caused me to miss a whole dimension of blessing that God wants to bestow on his children right now.

As we will see, God doesn't just take "guardianship" of children and give them new clothes; he creates new children that are in intimate union with him. God doesn't just take "ownership" of sinners while leaving them essentially unchanged; he actually makes them into new people; people that are part of the divine family. The old person is dead, a new person is alive. God doesn't just look at a believer as if they were a new person; they actually are a new person. Becoming a Christian involves not the covering of the old but the destruction of the old. It is the annihilation of satanic powers and flesh that enslaved us and the creation of a new person intimately connected to God. It is to become as united to God as biological children are to their parents, only more so. Becoming a Christian is to become a new baby in Christ.

Also, the "one time legal transaction" view of salvation fails to take into account the long process of growth and development that follows the initial gift of new life. God doesn't just make babies, he grows children to maturity. Put another way (and to use another of the salvation models we discussed above,) God doesn't just sign people up and then leave them to do whatever they want until he returns; he calls men and women into discipleship. To become a Christian is to leave everything and follow Jesus into a long journey and a hard battle. My view of salvation was faulty largely because I didn't realize that salvation is more than a one time act.

So how does this work? What does it mean to die and be created again and how does God accomplish it? Also, what does it mean to be a disciple of God? And where does the Exodus story fit into all this? To begin to answer those questions we will start with the Red Sea crossing (Exodus 13:17-14:31).

The miraculous deliverance through the Red sea was a pivotal event in Israel's history. It involved the final defeat of the armies of Egypt and as such was the point at which the Hebrews first became a truly free people. I want to focus on two interesting aspects of this story that give us insight into the nature of God and his plan of redemption and that helped me understand where my understanding of salvation fell short.

A New Creation

One Man and Water: A Creation Pattern
The first involves the nature of the Red Sea event. As unique as it is, even in biblical times, to have God part a body of water with wind so people can walk through on dry ground, several features of the crossing are quite typical of God's action in history. In examining the similarities between the Red Sea crossing and some other major acts of God, we can better understand why God chose to use this method to free his people and what it meant when he did.

I am going to suggest that the Red Sea was the point at which the Israelites were given new life. On one side of the water they were "dead:" although they were on the run, in a very real sense they still belonged to the Pharaoh and his army. However, on the other side they were newly "alive:" the Pharaoh had been defeated and they were now a new people. God had defeated evil and created for himself (again) a son. Israel had been born again. The reason I think we can speak about the Red Sea crossing in this way is that God had already established a very clear pattern in history into which the Red Sea episode fits well. God had shown that he is the destroyer of sin and the creator of life, and he had been remarkably consistent in the means by which he does these things. Specifically, God had shown in both the original creation of the universe (Gen. 1) and the flood (Gen. 6) that he uses water to judge sin and bring forth new life and that this creation involves the growth of a family from one special man. In the first few chapters of the Bible, God reveals that he does not disregard sin or give it a new covering. When his creation rebels against him, God destroys the evil and creates anew. Through the water comes life and death and from one man comes descendents of God; a righteous line. That is exactly what God does at the Exodus.

I will set the stage for that episode by quickly surveying God's work at the creation of the universe and the flood. Then we will see how the Exodus fits into God's pattern and follow that by showing how God used the same model in Jesus and how he continues to do so even today.

Adam and the Creation of the Universe

According to Genesis 1, in the beginning there was formlessness, darkness, and water. Traditionally, this has been understood as a state of lifeless disorder. The Spirit of God hovers over the proceedings and, as the Spirit works, the Earth is gradually turned from a chaotic wasteland to a well ordered planet brimming with life. This action involved both judgment and creation.

The life-giving aspect is obvious, as the Spirit draws life out the water and we end up with not only with plants and animals, but the crown of creation: God's first human children, Adam and Eve. They are the father and mother of the family of God on Earth. Through one man, then, God has created descendents for himself.

The destructive part of the original creation is perhaps not so obvious to modern Western readers, but there is a strong interpretative tradition that understands creation to be the bringing of order out of the chaos of the water. Theologians have long viewed the creation narrative as the story of God's victory over the sea dragon Leviathan which represents death.[7] As Pete Enns notes,

> One of the ways the Old Testament describes creation is through a conflict between Yahweh and the sea (or "waters" or one of the sea monsters, Leviathan or Rahab). Sea is a symbol of chaos, and so Yahweh's victory in the conflict establishes order. He is the creator, the supreme power. Israel's proper response is awe and praise.

Enns points out that this "cosmic Battle" motif in regards to creation was common in the ancient Near East and would have been very familiar to the Israelites. It is clearly displayed in several other places in scripture. For example:

- Psalm 104:7: "at your rebuke the waters fled." This is not talking about low tide at the beach. Without raising a hand, the waters scampered away and were defeated.

- Psalm 89:9-10: Yahweh rules "over the surging sea" and "crushed Rahab."
- Job 9:13: the "cohorts of Rahab cowered" at Yahweh's feet.
- Psalm 74:13-14: Yahweh "split open sea...broke the heads of the monster in the waters...crushed the heads of Leviathan."
- Psalm 77:16, when the waters saw God coming, they went into a panic attack: they "writhed and convulsed." [8]

The Israelites clearly associated the sea with the evil forces that God works to defeat. That is one of the reasons that Jesus calming the storm (Mark 4:35-41) was such a big deal, and why the final act of creation, the New Heaven and Earth, will have no sea (Revelation 21:1). But I am getting ahead of myself! For now I just want to emphasize that the creation of the world involved using water both to bring life through one man and to destroy death. As we will see, the exact same thing can be said about the great flood.

Noah and the Flood
   Adam and Eve rebelled against God and their descendents became more and more evil (Gen. 3-4). God decided to act. Interestingly, he did not give the people a quick and easy legal way out. He did not offer them a free ticket to Heaven if they would believe some facts about him. He did not decide to pick a few people and view them as righteous rather than as sinful. Instead, he simply wiped them out and started all over again. God created the world for a second time. He sent water to destroy sin and through the water he also brought life in the form of one man and his descendents. Noah was the second Adam and the flood was a second act of

creation. I think we see this clearly in the overall narrative, but also in some of the specific literary clues and historical parallels between the two accounts. For example, the flood begins when "the springs of the great deep burst forth" (Genesis 7:11). The word for deep is the same used in Genesis 1:2 to describe the initial watery condition of earth.

Also, there is an emphasis on the number seven in the flood story: Noah is to take seven pairs of clean animals (Genesis 7:2), he is in the ark for seven days before the flood begins (Genesis 7:4), and a dove is sent every seven days to search for land (Genesis 8:10-12).

As for that dove, the fact that it hovers over the water is reminiscent of the Spirit hovering over waters of deep in Genesis 1. What is its goal? To bring life (in the form of a branch) out of the water.

In regards to Noah, his relationship to Adam is made quite explicit in Genesis 9:1-2, where he is given dominion over the plants and animals and told to be fruitful and multiply. This, of course, is the role and command that God originally gave to Adam (Genesis 1:28). Noah was now the leader of God's family; he was the new Adam. Noah was the righteous man who would be the father of God's children. So the flood was not only judgment but also re-creation. At the flood, "the whole universe, soiled by the tide of sin, by the intervention of water was restored to its pristine purity"[9] and out of the water came a people of God, a new righteous line. That is also exactly what happened at the Red Sea crossing.

Moses and the Crossing of the Red Sea

I am going to suggest in this section that the Red Sea crossing was one more instance in which God used one special man to lead people through the water of destruction and out of it to new life, thus creating for himself a family. To set the stage for the drama at the Red Sea, though, and make my case stronger, I want to start by examining the account of the birth of that special man: Moses. I believe Moses' early childhood is the first aspect of the Exodus account that shows the connection between creation, the flood and the Red Sea. In it we will see that God followed the same pattern to bring about new life for Moses as he had previously used at the creation of the universe and at the flood

The man that God would use to deliver his people was born under a death sentence. The king of Egypt had ordered that all male Hebrew babies should be killed by being thrown into the Nile River (Exodus 1:22). Moses' mother protected him for three months, but when she could no longer hide him, she made a basket, put Moses in it, and placed it in the reeds along the bank of the Nile. At that time Pharaoh's daughter came down to the river to bathe, noticed the baby in the basket and took him home to raise him as her own. She named him Moses, which means "I drew him out of the water" (Exodus 2:1-10).

So Moses was born in a similar situation to the people of Earth at the time of the flood: decreed by the king to be killed by water. However, Moses, like Noah before him, escaped that judgment by entering into an ark. The same water that was a force of destruction to others became the source of life for Moses. Not only did he survive, but he was given royal sonship. Moses entered into the water a slave, but came out of it as a member of the king's family! There is a very real sense in which Moses was born again in that water. That is why he was given his name. He had been recreated, given new life by being drawn out of the water. Indeed, from an Egyptian perspective (they believed the king was a god,) Moses had been given divine life.

Therefore, Moses' birth story conforms to the model we have already seen at the creation of the universe and the flood: Moses is like Noah and like Adam. Indeed, at this point in the biblical story, he is God's latest new Adam. He is the leader of a family of God. Where is this family created? Based on God's pattern that has already been established to this point in the narrative, I think it is clear that new life is given to the people of God at the Red Sea. Just like Moses, they are born again as they are drawn out of the water.

Let's examine this more closely. Like Moses, the Israelites were also in a similar position to the people of Earth before the flood: they were under penalty of death; part of a sinful culture that was under God's judgment. However, the link between the situation of the Israelites in slavery and humanity at the time of the flood is even more explicit. As I wrote in the introduction, the problems of the Israelites in Egypt are allegorically the problems of all mankind since the fall of Adam. They were separated from their true home, in slavery to the Pharaoh, and under God's judgment for worshipping false gods. The people before the flood were separated from God, in slavery to sin and Satan, and under God's judgment for worshiping false gods. It is the same situation we face today, by the way. (More on that later.)

The parallels between the Red Sea and the flood continue in the way the people were saved. Like those who followed Noah into the ark and through the water before them, the Israelites who followed Moses through the waters of the Red Sea were spared. Also, the same water that provided new life to the Israelites was the source of death to the Egyptians who opposed them. The Red Sea was the final judgment on the false gods of Egypt and the rebellious people (Exodus 6:6; 12:12). Again, God granted life and destroyed evil with the same water.

Before moving on to how this pattern continues right up until our day, let's pause and point out again that God did not "save" his people by simply forgiving them. He gave them a new existence. God didn't just grant the people a cloak of righteousness; he took them through the water to make them a new, holy people.

This is not the end of the story, of course. Moses and the Israelites are types. They show us how God works and foreshadow his ultimate purpose, which is to create a spiritual and eternal family. He does this through a man who is like Moses in many ways: Jesus.

Similarities between Moses and Jesus

By now I suspect that you can see where I am going with this: Jesus is our new Adam. He is like Noah and Moses in that he is the one who leads us through the water to new life. For our purposes, I will focus mostly on Jesus' similarities to Moses, starting with a few historical parallels in their lives. I believe God providentially caused these similarities to help us realize that Moses is a type of Christ. When we understand that Jesus is like Moses, we can better understand what Jesus accomplished in his ministry. I will then apply this principle by discussing how Jesus was like Moses in his ministry. Finally, I will examine ways to appropriate Jesus' work in our lives today.

The first similarity between Moses and Jesus involves the circumstances of their birth. Moses was born into an oppressed people living under an evil tyrant who tried to have him killed. So was Jesus. Just like the Pharaoh centuries before him, King Herod was concerned about someone rising up to take his throne (Matthew 2:3-6). He heard that a "King of the Jews" had been born and, in order to quell an uprising before it started, he ordered that all Hebrew babies two years old and younger be killed (Matthew 2:16). Jesus' parents fled to Egypt, where they stayed until Herod died (Matthew 2:14-15).

Another aspect of Moses' life that points toward Jesus is the fact that he gave up his position of honor and privilege to identify with the people he loved. Moses was a powerful prince, but he became a nobody, a shepherd herding flocks in the middle of nowhere. The writer of Hebrews describes his action this way: "By faith Moses, when he had grown up, refused to be known as the son of Pharaoh's daughter. He chose to be mistreated along with the people of God rather than to enjoy the pleasures of sin for a short time" (Hebrews 11:24-25).

In the same spirit as Moses, Jesus gave up his position in Heaven in order to identify with the people he loved. Paul portrays Jesus in these glowing terms: "Who, being in very nature God, did not consider equality with God something to be grasped, but made himself nothing, taking the very nature of a servant, being made in human likeness. And being found in appearance as a man, he humbled himself and became obedient to death – even death on a cross!" (Philippians 2:6-8).

Here is another similarity: when Moses came to lead his people, most didn't welcome him with open arms. Pharaoh responded to Moses' first demand to let the people go by making their work even harder, which resulted in the Hebrews cursing Moses for bringing more trouble on them (Exodus 5:19-21).

In the same way, Jesus was "despised and rejected by men, a man of sorrows, and familiar with suffering. Like one from whom men hide their faces he was despised, and we esteemed him not" (Isaiah 53:3). John explains that "he came to that which was his own, but his own did not receive him" (John 1:11). Jesus came to set humanity free, but most people weren't interested. Rather than follow, they called for his crucifixion.

Belonging to Two Families

Moses and Jesus had remarkably similar experiences that should make us ponder the link between the two men. However, perhaps the strongest illustrative parallel between Moses and Jesus is the unique family ties that each possessed. Both Moses and Jesus were members of two families, one royal and one common, and these multiple connections were necessary to complete their redemptive mission.

As we discussed above, Moses was born a Jew but was adopted into the Egyptian ruling family. As a Hebrew he was able to relate to the people and exercise the authority necessary to lead them; it seems unlikely they would have followed a non-Israelite. On the other hand, as a member of the Pharaoh's family, Moses was granted the access necessary to enter the court and demand the slaves' release. It seems unlikely that he would have been able to do this if he did not have that connection. Moses needed to be both an Egyptian royal and an Israelite to accomplish his task.

In the same way, Jesus is a man but is also God. He was born to Mary in Bethlehem, but at the same time has always existed as part of the Godhead (John 1:1). As a member of the human family, he is able to relate to us and exercise the necessary authority to lead us home. As the Son of God, Jesus has access to the very throne room of God, so that he may make intercession for us (Romans 8:34). The fact that he was both God and man was and is absolutely essential to his goal.

God providentially placed Moses in the Pharaoh's family so, when the time was right, he would have access to the seat of power and secure the Jews' release. In this way, God illustrated what would later occur with

Jesus. I think this is another act that is typical of God, in that he also did a similar thing later in Israel's history with a young lady named Esther. Esther was also a type of Jesus in that she, too, was a member of two families who interceded with the king to save her people.

I won't tell the whole story here, but Esther was a Jewish girl who won a contest and became King Xerxes' queen (Esther 1-2). Xerxes did not know at the time that Esther was Jewish, so when Haman, a trusted nobleman close to the king, devised a plot to kill all the Jews in the land, Xerxes went along with it (Esther 3:6-15). Esther's cousin Mordecai convinced her that she had to do something to stop the annihilation of her people, and Esther bravely went before the king to intercede on their behalf (Esther 4:1-5:2). There are many more interesting twists and turns within the biblical account, but the bottom line is that Esther's plea was successful and the Jews were saved (Esther 5:3-9:17). Just as he had done with Moses, God providentially placed Esther in the royal family so she could have access to the seat of power when that became necessary to save the Israelites. Both Moses and Esther are people who illuminate Jesus, the human who has the membership in the divine royal family that is necessary to save us.

Jesus, Baptism, and the Creation of a Spiritual People of God

This unique nature is dramatically proclaimed and illustrated in one of the more striking and beautiful scenes in the New Testament: Jesus' baptism. Jesus comes to John and is baptized in the Jordan River. When he comes up out of the water, the Spirit of God in the form of a dove descends and lands on Jesus and a voice from Heaven proclaims "This is my Son!" (Matt. 3:13-17).

This is an amazing episode in that it brings together much of the imagery from this chapter. For example, the Spirit of God in the form of a dove over the river brings to mind both the initial creation account in which the Sprit hovered over the water, and the flood, in which the dove hovered over the water. As we discussed, in both cases the Spirit/dove brought life out of the water.

As for that life out of the water, we have also seen that in the case of creation, the flood, Moses birth, and the Red Sea crossing, God brought "divine" life out of the water. Moses was drawn out of the water to be part of the royal family, and in the other cases God brought entire groups out of the water to be part of his family. In the case of Jesus, there is no need for quotation marks around the word divine. Jesus actually is God. He was not made God at his baptism (that heresy was condemned early in Church history) but his status as God's son was officially pronounced to the world as he came out of the water. At this we also see his status as the new Moses, the new Noah, and the new Adam.

In fact, Jesus is not only the latest new Adam, but he is the last Adam! With Jesus, God's plan for creating a family of God through one special man finds fulfillment and completion. The first Adam was physical (as were his subsequent types Noah and Moses, as well as their descendents) but, as Paul teaches, Jesus is a spiritual Adam:

> So it is written: "The first man Adam became a living being"; the last Adam, a life-giving spirit. The spiritual did not come first, but the natural, and after that the spiritual. The first man was of the dust of the earth, the second man from heaven. As was the earthly man, so are those who are of the earth; and as is the man from heaven, so also are those who are of heaven. And just as we have

borne the likeness of the earthly man, so shall we bear the likeness of the man from heaven. (1 Cor. 15-49)

Jesus had divine life and those who follow him are given divine life as well! Jesus is the head of the final righteous line of God. Those that become a part of God's family are not simply forgiven or granted a new legal status, they are re-created.

That is why the entrance rite of the Church has always been baptism. We enter the baptismal water under God's judgment and as slaves to sin and to Satan; we come out of it as free children of God. Fulfilling the action of the flood and the Red Sea, our evil nature is destroyed in the water and we are granted new life. These connections between the flood, the Red Sea crossing, and baptism are explicitly made by Peter in 1 Peter 3:21 and Paul in 1 Corinthians 10:2.

A New Creation

The point of this very brief historical survey of God's pattern of granting new life is to emphasize that salvation involves God making us into new people, not just giving us a whitewash. When Jesus told Nicodemus that he must be born again to enter the kingdom of God (John 3:3), he actually meant it. He wasn't talking about giving Nicodemus new legal standing as a member of God's family. He wasn't talking about painting over Nicodemus the sinner with a "righteousness covering." Jesus actually meant that Nicodemus needed to die and be created again by God.

When I realized this, my attitude toward sin started to change. I could no longer accept living a mediocre life in which sin still largely had control. If God had made me new, I needed to start living like it. This is exactly Paul's point in much of his ethical teaching. He spends a lot of time in the beginning of his letters establishing the nature of our new identity, saying things such as, "If anyone is in Christ he is a new creation; the old has gone, the new has come!" (2 Corinthians 5:17). He then follows that with an exhortation to live accordingly. For example, this passage from the first half of Ephesians establishes that we are new creations:

> As for you, you were dead in your transgressions and sins, in which you used to live when you followed the ways of this world and of the ruler of the kingdom of the air, the spirit who is now at work in those who are disobedient. All of us also lived among them at one time, gratifying the cravings of our sinful nature and following its desires and thoughts. Like the rest, we were by nature objects of wrath. But because of his great love for us, God, who is rich in mercy, made us alive with Christ even when we were dead in transgressions—it is by grace you have been saved. (Ephesians 2:1-5)

We were dead and now we are alive! It reminds me of what the father said to the prodigal son when he returned: "This son of mine was dead and is alive again" (Luke 15:24). The implications of this truth are spelled out in the last half of Ephesians. They include this instruction:

> You were taught, with regard to your former way of life, to put off your old self, which is being corrupted by its deceitful desires; to be made new in the attitude of your minds; and to put on the new self, created to be like God in true righteousness and holiness. (Ephesians 4:22-24)

So we are a new creation, one that is intended to actually be righteous and holy. We simply cannot be satisfied with not being so. If we are children of God, something really has changed about us. It is not just a new label, but a new reality. When God has children, he is not giving orphans new names or drafting an expansion team, but actually bearing new babies.

As we will discuss throughout this book, God's ultimate intent is to have a family of mature adults, living together as the Trinity lives together. God's first step in that process is to create new life.

So, then, we need to ask ourselves: how are we living? As a person who has simply been forgiven or a person whom God has created anew? Do we live like we have actually been born again? As John declares, those who do not live like a child of God in more than a legal sense need to question whether they truly are children of God: "This is how we know who the children of God are and who the children of the devil are: Anyone who does not do what is right is not a child of God: nor is anyone who does not love his brother" (1 John 3:10)

A Journey and a Battle

The second aspect of the Red Sea crossing that caused me to adjust my view of salvation is related to the first. As I mentioned, I had viewed redemption as primarily a one time legal transaction. In the first part of this chapter I discussed how I was wrong about it simply being legal. It is more than that: it is the creation of new life. In this section I will focus on the notion of salvation as a one-time event. Even if we understand properly the concept of being born again, we might be tempted to focus on that amazing occurrence as the end all and be all of salvation. However, that would be as silly as thinking that having children is only about the moment of birth.

Of course it isn't. Parenting isn't simply about bringing kids into existence. It is about guiding them to maturity. That is what God does with his children as well. God doesn't just grant life, he desires to see that life develop and grow. That is far from a one time event. Rather, it is a long and often difficult process. That is what I want to emphasize here. Again, the Red Sea event gives us insight into this aspect of God's redemptive plan.

In my former view of salvation, I basically defined it as the point at which I "made a decision for Christ." Using the Exodus as a model for redemption, I would have equated this with the point at which the Israelites marched out of Egypt under the blood of the lamb. The Passover would be the point of salvation and everything after that is just something extra but not necessary. However, as I studied the Exodus and realized it is a model for salvation, it was interesting to me that the story did not end after the Passover, or even after the Red Sea. Rather, these events were just the beginning of the story. They were the starting point of salvation, not its entirety.[10]

God wanted more than a one-time decision from the Hebrews. He did not treat the act of putting blood over the door as an automatic ticket into the Promised Land. He did not want just one night of obedience. Instead he wanted a lifetime of walking in close relationship with him. Only this would actually get the Israelites into Canaan.

I believe this speaks to a truth about the nature of salvation. It is not a one time decision, but a lifetime of following Jesus. It is less like a business transaction and more like a journey and a battle. It is less like receiving a ticket to Heaven and more like trying to get across a wilderness.

If the Red Sea represented the totality of salvation, I think we could have expected to see something along these lines: God should immediately (or at least very quickly) have plopped the Children of Israel down in the Promised Land, as they had accomplished his entrance requirements. At the very least he should have handed out "Get into Canaan Free" cards and told the people to present them at the border when they arrived. Neither of those things happened. There was no Star Trek-like transporter to beam the Israelites up out of Egypt as soon as they trusted God by placing the blood over their doors. We don't read of them being re-animated instantly inside the Promised Land as soon as they reached the far side of the Red Sea. Also, God didn't tell them to just go and find their own way in life, waiting for the Promised Land to be ready for them.

Instead, God led the Israelites hour by hour. He guided them using a cloud by day and fire by night. Rather than tell the people to go it on their own, he demanded that they fall in line behind him and submit to his direction. They weren't to make a move without being directed by the Lord: "In all the travels of the Israelites, whenever the cloud lifted from above the tabernacle, they would set out; but if the cloud did not lift, they did not set out – until the day it lifted" (Exodus 40:36-37).

The Passover and exit from Egypt was not the complete salvation experience. It was just the first step. It was the beginning of a long journey lived in submission to God's plan; the start of an endurance race and a hard battle. God called the Israelites to follow him – to place their hopes and dreams in his hands and submit their will to his until they finally arrived at home.

The Narrow Road

The understanding of salvation as a life of discipleship lines up well with the gospels. Jesus did not go around offering "Get into Heaven Free" cards. He did not implore his listeners to make a one-time decision that would seal the deal forever. Rather, he called men and women to follow him, to submit their hopes and dreams to him, to become his disciples.

The Israelites came out of Egypt armed to fight and ready to walk, because God had called them to a battle and a journey. That is exactly the same call of Jesus. He says, "Enter through the narrow gate. For wide is the gate and broad is the road that leads to destruction, and many enter through it. But small is the gate and narrow the road that leads to life, and only a few find it" (Matthew 7:13-14).

Notice that the gate is just a starting point. It opens to the road, on which we spend our Christian life traveling. Jesus' call is not just to believe that he is God or make a spiritual decision of some kind (although it certainly includes both), but rather it is to give up your will to his and follow him. We give more examples of this when we discuss the radical and sacrificial nature of Jesus' call in the next chapter. For now, let me point out that the idea of salvation as a journey (or a race) and a battle is not just found in the gospels. The rest of the New Testament is filled with similar imagery. Followers of Jesus are continually referred to as soldiers and athletes. For example, the church in Corinth is encouraged with these words:

> Do you not know that in a race all the runners run, but only one gets the prize? Run in such a way as to get the prize. Everyone who competes in the games goes into strict training. They do it to get a crown that will not last; but we do it to get a

crown that will last forever. Therefore I do not run like a man running aimlessly; I do not fight like a man beating the air. No, I beat my body and make it my slave so that after I have preached to others, I myself will not be disqualified for the prize. (1 Corinthians 9:24-27)

Paul questions the Galatians using similar language: "You were running a good race. Who cut in on you and kept you from obeying the truth?" (Galatians 5:7). On a more military note, the Ephesians are told to "Put on the full armor of God so that you can take your stand against the devil's schemes. For our struggle is not against flesh and blood, but against the rulers, against the authorities, against the powers of this dark world and against the spiritual forces of evil in the heavenly realms (Ephesians 6:11-12).

As is clear from that passage, "Though we live in the world, we do not wage war as the world does. The weapons we fight with are not the weapons of the world. On the contrary, they have divine power to demolish strongholds" (2 Corinthians 10:3-4). Peter warns: "Be self-controlled and alert. Your enemy the devil prowls around like a roaring lion looking for someone to devour. Resist him, standing firm in the faith, because you know that your brothers throughout the world are undergoing the same kind of sufferings" (1 Peter 5:8-9). With that in mind, young pastor Timothy is told: "Fight the good fight of the faith. Take hold of the eternal life to which you were called when you made your good confession in the presence of many witnesses" (1 Timothy 6:12).

In the second letter to Timothy, Paul explains further that his apprentice should, "Endure hardship with us like a good soldier of Christ Jesus. No one serving as a soldier gets involved in civilian affairs – he wants to please his commanding officer. Similarly, if anyone competes as an athlete, he does not receive the victor's crown unless he competes according to the rules" (2 Timothy 2:3-5). The fact that the Christian life is a race and a battle is clear. Salvation is not a one-time act, nor is it a free pass to do whatever you want with your life until Jesus takes you to Heaven. It is a radical call to give up everything and follow Jesus, joining his army as travels and fights its way across the wilderness to the Promised Land. Rather than a summons to sign your name on boring theological treatise, the call of Jesus is an invitation to a marvelous adventure.

At the very end of his life, Paul, who constantly referred to himself as a "slave of Christ" (Romans 1:1, Philippians 1:1 and Titus 1:1, for example), looks ahead to finally arriving in Heaven. He doesn't say, "I'm glad I've got my entry card" or "I hope Jesus remembers me from that one time that we met." Instead he says, "I have fought the good fight, I have finished the race, I have kept the faith" (2 Timothy 4:7). May that be our testimony as well.

Chapter 2

Sacrifice

Does God Want Us to Give Up Some Stuff?
As a young twenty-something, I faced what felt like the biggest decision of my life to that point: Should I move from Canada to California to attend Bible College and work with an inner-city mission agency? I had recently become serious about following Jesus and was quite convinced that God wanted me to go. However, I struggled immensely with the decision because of all that I would have to give up. Although I was extremely excited about moving, I was very reluctant to leave friends and family. On top of that, I had been offered a job on the oil rigs of northern Alberta. Money was scarce for me at the time and this represented a chance to make some really good cash. What should I do? I must admit, I was very tempted to stay in Canada and work. However, after much prayer and thought, I decided to decline the high paying job and move. Looking back, it was definitely the right thing to do and I have never regretted my decision for a second. However, it sure was a tough call at the time and frankly, I was quite confused about it.

The reason for this was that I simply didn't understand the notion of sacrifice. My experience suggested to me that God actually wanted sacrifice, but that just didn't seem right; I didn't think I should have to do it. I wanted to serve God without giving up anything. For example, it occurred to me that God should let me win the lottery (or come into a pile of money some other way) so that I could pay for all my college and not have to think about it. Or, I wondered, why couldn't I find a field of service closer to home? Basically, I wanted to have my cake and eat it too.

In retrospect, I think this was a somewhat natural response given that we live in a culture that despises the idea of sacrifice. I had been bombarded (as we all are) with the idea that that life is all about getting as much as you can, as fast as you can, for as little effort as you can. This is even the attitude in many of our churches. Christianity is often presented as an easy way to get all the earthly blessings that God wants to give you. If it is even mentioned at all, sacrifice is seen as an outmoded form of worship that we don't need to bother with today. Sacrifice is seen as something for the Old Testament, but we live in New Testament times now, so we can ignore it. With these ideas rattling around in my head, I couldn't figure out why God wanted me to sacrifice.

I have since learned that he had very good reasons for doing so. In fact, they are some of the same reasons God has always wanted sacrifice. The fact is that sacrifice has been integral to God's relationship with man since the very beginning and continues to be so today. While it is true that we don't have to sacrifice animals anymore, God has not changed and the purposes for which God requires sacrifice have not changed. As we examine how God used sacrifice in the Israelites escape from Egypt, we will see some of those reasons. Before we get back to the Exodus, though, I want to lay a foundation for that discussion by briefly exploring the relationship between love and sacrifice.

Love and Sacrifice

My argument in this chapter is going to be that God requires sacrifice because he loves us and wants us to love him. Sacrifice is integral to that relationship. Before making that case, though, I think we need to define one aspect of what the Bible means by love. It is far different than our common usage. In our culture, the concept of love centers on emotions and subjective value judgments. It is generally understood that to love someone is to have nice feelings about them. To say, "I love you" is usually to mean, "Thinking about you generates pleasurable feelings inside of me." This is why people fall in and out of love so quickly. When the feelings fade, they equate that with a loss of love. They "no longer have feelings" for the other person. This understanding of love is not biblical. In scripture, love does not refer primarily to an emotional state. Rather, to love biblically is to act in a self-sacrificing way for the good of others.

For example, Jesus' most famous teaching on love took place on the day before his crucifixion. After washing his disciples' feet and explaining that he was going to be betrayed and would have to leave them, he said, "A new command I give you: Love one another. As I have loved you, so you must love one another. By this all men will know that you are my disciples, if you love one another" (John 13:34-35).

How did Jesus define love? What did he mean when he said the disciples should love each other in the same way that Jesus loved them? The broader context of this passage in John is one in which Jesus, the Creator and King of the Universe, not only stooped to wash his disciples' feet, but then gave up his very life that they might be saved. To love as Jesus loved, then, is to act self-sacrificially. The disciples were instructed to sacrifice for others. When Jesus repeated the commandment later, he made this plain. "My command is this: Love each other as I have loved you. Greater love has no one than this, that he lay down his life for his friends" (John 15:12-13). John obviously looks back at this teaching as he explains the meaning of love in the first of his epistles.

> This is the message you heard from the beginning: We should love one another. ... This is how we know what love is: Jesus Christ laid down his life for us. And we ought to lay down our lives for our brothers. If anyone has material possessions and sees his brother in need but has no pity on him, how can the love of God be in him? Dear children, let us not love with words or tongue but with actions and in truth. (1 John 3:11, 16-18)

Biblical love is more than nice words and pleasant feelings. It is sacrificial action. When the Bible talks about God loving us, it is primarily speaking of the fact that he acts in a self-sacrificing way for our benefit.

The most famous verse in the Bible, John 3:16, is no exception. When John says, "God so loved the world that he gave his one and only Son," we shouldn't read it, "God felt such overwhelming feelings of affection for us that he wanted to do more than just send flowers, so he sent his only son." Rather, it should read "God loved the world in this extraordinary way: he sent his son to die for us." The act of sending his son to die is an example of God's self-sacrificial action for our good. That is Paul's point in Romans 5:8: "God demonstrates his own love for us in this: While we were still sinners, Christ died for us."

Does God have affectionate feelings for us? Of course. But we shouldn't allow our culture's cheap romanticism override the biblical view of love. Love, according to scripture, is not the emotion high school students feel when they catch sight of their latest flame walking across the parking lot. It is not defined by feelings at all. Rather, love is self-giving action for the good of another. To love someone, then, is to sacrifice for their benefit. If we are unwilling to sacrifice for someone, it is a sign that we do not love them.

To flesh that out a bit more, to sacrifice for someone is to demonstrate that you consider whatever it is that you are sacrificing to be of less value than the person for whom you are sacrificing. On the other hand, if we refuse to sacrifice for someone, it shows that we value whatever it is we refuse to sacrifice to be of greater value than the person.

This principle of reality is something we know instinctively, I think, and those that want to have successful relationships learn to practice it even if they have never articulated it. For example, the other day a recently married friend was telling me about how his life had changed since the nuptials. He explained that he had decided to give up watching basketball because it took away from the already limited time he got to spend with his wife. (They both worked full time.) Actually, he clarified, he no longer watched regular season basketball. His wife had suggested that he should still watch the playoffs because, while she agreed that giving up basketball was good for their relationship, she knew he really enjoyed the games and didn't want him to miss them all. This is an everyday example of love. He sacrificed basketball because he valued his wife; his wife sacrificed some time with him during the playoffs because she valued her husband. When I made this observation to him in the conversation, he replied that it never occurred to him to think of it that way. He was simply loving his wife, not thinking about sacrifice. Indeed.

The principle also holds true in other aspects of family life. My wife and I just had our fourth child, and if getting married is like attending the University of How to Learn to Sacrifice, then having kids is Ph.D.

level work. Parenting is all about sacrifice. From changing dirty diapers to paying for college, parents give of themselves for their children. But like my friend, I don't concentrate on the fact that I am sacrificing. I just love my kids. Certainly strong emotions are part of that love, but at a basic level, it is largely about sacrifice.

God, Love, and the Purpose of Life
One more thing before we get to the Exodus again. The Bible says not only that God loves us, but that God *is* love. We have talked about how God sacrifices for our good ("loves us",) but what does it mean that he is love?

I think at least part of the answer is the fact that God has existed in a mutually self-giving relationship within the Trinity forever. The Trinity is the three persons of the Godhead giving of themselves to each other. Love is the essence of God's existence. I point this out because that means that love is the most basic "thing" in all of reality. As Danielou writes, "Without a doubt the master-key to Christian theology... is contained in the statement that the Trinity of Persons constitutes the structure of Being, and that love is therefore as primary as existence" [11] Because God is love, love is what creation is all about.

Put another way, we exist to love God and love each other. That is our ultimate purpose in life and it is the end for which God works. As Jesus said, all the commandments are summed up in two lines: "Love the Lord your God with all your heart and with all your soul and with all your mind" and "Love your neighbor as yourself" (Matthew 22:37-38).

Given that the purpose of life is love and to love is to give of ourselves for the good of others, we can accurately say that we were created for sacrifice.

At its core, sin is a refusal to do that. Humanity's fall was and is a failure to love God. What happened in the garden? Adam and Eve saw that the apple was good for food, pleasing to the eye, and desirable for gaining wisdom and they decided that they wanted those things more than God. They would not sacrifice temporal, worldly benefit for eternal relationship with God. They decided to worship and serve the created thing rather than the creator, which is what we all do (Rom 1:25). Practically speaking, we value ourselves and our earthly pleasure above all and, as a result, are unwilling to give of ourselves for God or anyone else. We refuse to love. That is our foundational problem. What God needs to do, then, is teach us to love.

Learning to Love

Again, family life gives us a good picture of this process. Children are not naturally self-giving. Quite the opposite in fact; they are born with a penchant for pride and selfishness. They have to learn to love. In my experience, this happens primarily in two ways: 1. By example and 2. Through rules.

I have wonderful parents and I grew up watching them give and give and give for others. They dedicated their lives to their children and to the spreading of the gospel and I have tried to model their example. As I do, I realize that they are the ones who showed me what it is to love.

However, it wasn't just their example. They also had rules. My sisters and I weren't given voluntary guidelines about how to play together or divide our toys: we were forced to share. I am very thankful for that now, and I enforce the same rules on my kids. They either share their toys with each other (and every so often give some of them away to kids who don't have any) or they don't get to play with them. In this way I am trying to guide my children toward being loving people. I don't want them to grow up to be self centered, egotistical brats. More specifically, I don't want them to grow up valuing themselves or their toys and games more than their siblings. One of the main points of being forced to share is that the kids get it in their heads that other people are more important than toys and that we should value the other person's experience more than our own. By forcing them to give up some time with the doll or the race car, I am trying to help them see that the other person is more important than either of those items, as fun as each may be.

God uses the same type of techniques in teaching us how to love. 1. He demonstrates love to us by sacrificing for us and 2. He puts rules in place that are intended to push us toward placing the proper value on things. That is where all the rules about sacrifice come in. They are intended to teach us to love God and break us from our love for everything that is not God. Sacrifice is not commanded because God needs what we have to offer. Rather, we need to give it to him. We see clearly how this works in the Exodus story.

Sacrifice and the Exodus

The requirement to sacrifice was the original reason the Israelites were to leave Egypt. When Moses told Pharaoh to let God's people go, he explained that it was so the Hebrews could go sacrifice in the desert (Exodus 7:16). After the plague of flies, Pharaoh said he would allow the Israelites to worship, but only within the land of Egypt. Moses refused the offer, explaining that the sacrifices that the Israelites were going to offer would be detestable to the Egyptians and cause an attack on the Israelites (Exodus 8:25-26). What Moses is saying is that the Hebrews will be sacrificing animals that the Egyptians venerate.

Egypt was a land of many gods, somewhat similar to India today. And also like modern India, certain animals were considered holy. I have travelled to India several times and one of the first things you notice is that cattle have a lot of freedom to roam. That is because in Hinduism, cattle (and other animals) are venerated. As such, when I am in India, I do not suggest to the people that we lasso a wandering cow and slaughter it for the evening meal. That is the principle that Moses is applying here. He does not want to sacrifice within sight of the Egyptians because he knows that the animals being sacrificed are holy to them.

Why would God command the Israelites to sacrifice animals that were worshiped by the Egyptians? Because the Israelites were worshiping them too and God wanted to break them of their idolatry! Israel had turned away from the one true God to worship foreign powers and now God was attempting to bring them back to him. (See Joshua 24:14-18, 1 Samuel 12 and Exodus 20:7 for explicit references to the fact that the Israelites were idolaters in Egypt.) By commanding the Hebrews to sacrifice the animals that they had previously worshiped, God is 1. Showing them that those beasts are not truly gods and 2. Placing them in a position where they have to give up what is less valuable for what is more valuable. Sacrificing the animals to the one true God puts them back in touch with reality; it orders the universe correctly.

As a bit of a side note here, I want to briefly point out that one of the major reasons for the plagues and the requirement to sacrifice was that God was judging the gods of Egypt. He was showing everyone that they were nothing compared to Him.

For example, the Nile River was viewed as a divine source of life in Egypt. It was worshiped because it was understood to determine the welfare of the people by providing necessary water for man, animals and crops. At God's command, however, it became a source of death (Exodus 17:14-24). God showed that he had authority over the river and that the God of Moses is the ultimate source of life, not the Nile.

As the plagues progressed, the defeat of the Egyptian gods (such as cattle in Exodus 9:1-7) continued and the demarcation between the God of Israel and the gods of Egypt became clearer. With the ninth plague, God brought "darkness that [could] be felt" (Exodus 10:21). Many scholars believe this was to demonstrate God's power over even the highest deity in Egypt, the sun god Ra.

It is important to note here, that God is showing not only the Egyptians that he is God over all other powers; he is showing the Israelites too! To return to the subject of sacrifice, then, we must realize that the reason for God's command to sacrifice is the need of the Israelites to renounce the Egyptian idolatry to which they were attached. This can also be deduced from several episodes in their subsequent wilderness journey.

For instance, soon after crossing the Red Sea, the Israelites complained because they had nothing to eat. God graciously provided them with manna (Exodus 16:1-5). Interestingly, in Exodus 12:28 it says that the Israelites left Egypt with large herds and flocks. Why were they not eating the cattle and sheep? Could it be that they refused to kill them due to the fact that they still considered them holy?

That thesis becomes all the more reasonable when we consider later incidents such as the building of the golden calf. Moses had given the people the Ten Commandments, the first two of which are "You shall have no other gods before me" and "You shall not make for yourself an idol in the form of heaven above or in the earth beneath or in the waters below" (Exodus 20:3-4). (Why would these be the first two rules? Because the biggest problem the people have is that they are idolaters!) The people readily agreed to these rules, but before their vow of obedience has finished echoing around the desert floor, they are back to worshipping Egyptian idols! While Moses was back up on Mt. Sinai, the people convinced Aaron to form for them an idol of gold, which they proceeded to worship (Exodus 32). I recently visited the Egyptian Museum in Cairo. There are golden calves all over the place. In erecting this idol, the Israelites were clearly going back to their Egyptian ways. The people had come out of Egypt, but God had not yet got Egypt out of his people.

So what did God do? He gave them specific and mandatory rules for sacrifices which addressed their penchant for loving someone other than God.

We see an example of this in the instructions for the Day of Atonement. Aaron the High Priest was told to make two sin offerings; a young bull for himself (Lev. 16:6; 11) and a goat for the people (Lev. 16:5). The calf for Aaron makes sense because of the golden calf incident. God is specifically making a point to Aaron about worshipping cattle. But what about the requirement of a goat for the rest of the people? Well, we see in the next chapter that God commands the people to stop worshipping "goat idols" (or "goat demons" (Lev 17:7). It seems that while Moses was teaching the priestly code to Levites for 12 weeks (the first half of Leviticus,) the people were making offerings to some kind of goat idols. While the sacrifice of a goat at Yom Kippur was for all sins (16:16), it would have sent a specific message to the people at the time about not venerating goats.

God's commands about sacrifice were meant to break the people of their love for false gods and lead them to love the one true God. They were to give up something specific that they valued for the sake of someone they should value more. God didn't ask them to sacrifice ants or something else they didn't care about. He wanted them to give up the animal idols they were worshiping. Again, this is a common principle in relationships. It means nothing to sacrifice something that you don't value. It wouldn't have done my friend any good to give up going to the opera for his wife, because he doesn't enjoy going to the opera anyway. He had to give up something that he valued, basketball, for it to truly be a loving gesture.

As we discussed above, sin is the refusal to love God and to accept his love. It is the refusal to sacrifice to him and to receive his sacrifice. The commandments were given to help reverse that situation. We need to understand, then, that God's interest in asking for sacrifice is part of his overall plan to get us to love him rather than something or someone else. Although this is similar to my friend's basketball situation, it is far more serious: God's commands to Israel were like one spouse asking the other to stop cheating with prostitutes. To God, idolatry is adultery. In fact, that is just the language God used in many places, including Judg. 2:17, 8:27, and 1 Chron. 5:25.

Jesus' Sacrificial Call

What does this mean to us today? We no longer have to sacrifice animals, but the principle of sacrificing as an act of love still applies. In fact, because of Jesus' example of perfect submission and obedience in giving himself to the Father (Philippians 2:1-11) (doing what the first Adam failed to do), we now see clearly what those sacrifices were supposed to lead us to: presenting our complete selves as a living sacrifice to God (Romans 12:1). Sacrifice was never about God needing animals. It was about breaking down barriers between man and God, whatever they may be. Sacrificing ourselves to God means that we must give up anything and everything that might get in the way of our relationship with him.

God doesn't just want certain parts of our lives; for example a tithe and a couple of hours on Sunday morning. He wants all of us. As such, he will ask us to sacrifice specific things that are (or might become) idolatrous to us. It's not going to be the same for every person. Therefore, he might ask us for money, time, alcohol, the internet, a boyfriend or girlfriend or, in my experience above, a job and proximity to family.

Jesus exhibited this principle consistently in his ministry, starting with the first disciples:

> As Jesus was walking beside the Sea of Galilee, he saw two brothers, Simon called Peter and his brother Andrew. They were casting a net into the lake, for they were fishermen. "Come, follow me," Jesus said, "and I will make you fishers of men." At once they left their nets and followed him. Going on from there, he saw two other brothers, James son of Zebedee and his brother John. They were in a boat with their father Zebedee, preparing their nets. Jesus called them, and immediately they left the boat and their father and followed him. (Matthew 4:18-22)

In order to follow Jesus, Peter, James, and John left their nets and their family. That is no small commitment. Why would Jesus ask them to do that? Because even the blessings of job and family can be idolatrous. They can keep us from God. I have been saddened several times in my life by stories of young people who want to become missionaries or work in ministry or study theology but are thwarted at every turn by parents who want them to do something more "success" oriented with their lives. (Never mind that one does not get more success oriented than laying up treasure in Heaven, but again, more on that later.) It is frustrating to think that one's family could come between you and God, but that is exactly what Jesus said would happen:

> Do not suppose that I have come to bring peace to the earth. I did not come to bring peace, but a sword. For I have come to turn 'a man against his father, a daughter against her mother, a daughter-in-law against her mother-in-law – a man's enemies will be the members of his own household.'

> Anyone who loves his father or mother more than me is not worthy of me; anyone who loves his son or daughter more than me is not worthy of me; and anyone who does not take his cross and follow me is not worthy of me. Whoever finds his life will lose it, and whoever loses his life for my sake will find it. (Matthew 10:34-39)

Notice that Jesus frames the issues as one of love. Whoever does not give up everything, including family, is showing that they love this world more than they love God. An email from a listener to my podcast provides an excellent example of how Jesus teaching can be applied today:

> I enjoyed the talk on how to communicate with difficult nonbelievers. It has been a struggle for me my whole Christian life. I grew up in an atheist household. A very HOSTILE atheist household. Both my parents and my brother still are. They read books from Dawkins, Dennet, and Hitchens and bombard me with their emotional rants against

the Christian faith on a daily basis. It is very difficult for me. (Let me clarify what exactly is difficult for me. I do not have trouble answering their objections. I have difficulty getting them to take the answers seriously. The conversation ends with, "once you get as old as us, you will get to understand these things like we do." That's where my difficulty lies). They shake their heads, pat me on mine, and say that I will eventually grow up, become smart (they use the term bright), and leave a religion that teaches hate and intolerance. (They refuse to believe that the God of the Bible is a loving God).

The passage from Matthew 10:34-39 has hit me right in the face when I think about this difficulty. When I first read this passage, It was hard for me to accept. I thought, "How could Jesus come to cause strife in the family. How HORRIBLE! Why would he want to set a family against each other? That's not a very good thing for a moral teacher to do." Well, now that I have given my life to Christ, the meaning of that passage came to me at a very personal level. One I do not like. One that I prefer not to have. Jesus did not come to gloss over differences just for the sake of superficial harmony. Commitment in Jesus can divide a family. In my case it has.

This young man has decided to love God, which is the right decision because loving God is necessary for eternal life: "The man who loves his life will lose it, while the man who hates his life in this world will keep it for eternal life. Whoever serves me must follow me; and where I am, my servant also will be. My Father will honor the one who serves me" (John 12:25-26).

This is the point Jesus made to the wealthy young ruler when he asked what he needed to do to inherit eternal life. Jesus told him to "Sell everything you have and give to the poor, and you will have treasure in heaven. Then come, follow me" (Luke 18:22). The man refused, and Jesus warned that having money makes it very difficult to enter the kingdom of God.

Not Just the Big Stuff

Money is a big cause of idolatry, of course, but idols aren't always so glamorous or easily identifiable. They can be small things as well. I remember several incidents after arriving in California for school in which God continued to emphasize the sacrificial nature of following him. They mostly involved getting rid of the few worldly possessions I had left at the time. For example, after paying for classes, I realized that I didn't quite have enough money for books. What to do? Sell my most valuable piece of clothing (a jacket) to my roommate who had been admiring it since I arrived. A few months later I learned that I would not be able to keep my little sports car in California due to environmental restrictions, so back to Canada it went. Through it all, God taught me that he had to come first.

I talked about how sports became a potential source of problems between my friend and his wife. It can also do that between us and God. This point was first driven home to me in the fall of 1993, when I was asked to attend a missions meeting at church on the same night as game six of the World Series. I had to listen on my car radio as Joe Carter hit a walk-off home run in the ninth inning to win it for the Toronto Blue Jays. It may seem like a small thing (and it is), but at the time it had huge meaning for me. I really wanted to see that game, and I had to decide what was more important: baseball or telling people about Jesus.

Counting the Cost

As I mentioned above, there are many Christian "leaders" today who downplay or simply ignore the sacrificial nature of the Christian life. They try to make salvation as simple and easy as possible for people when evangelizing. They make no harsh demands and make no mention of the parts of Jesus' message that may make a person uncomfortable, instead emphasizing the more "positive" aspects of the gospel.

Jesus did exactly the opposite. Because he knew that sacrifice is essential to salvation, Jesus took care to make sure his listeners understood just how much discipleship would cost them. He didn't water down the message to make it more appealing. On the contrary, Jesus emphasized the difficulty of the charge. For example, one day "a teacher of the law came to him and said, 'Teacher, I will follow you wherever you go.' Jesus replied, 'Foxes have holes and birds of the air have nests, but the Son of Man has no place to lay his head.' Another disciple said to him, 'Lord, first let me go and bury my father.' But Jesus told him, 'Follow me, and let the dead bury their own dead' (Matthew 8:18-22).

The first man seemed eager to follow Jesus. He was what many would consider an ideal candidate for discipleship, a prototypical seeker. Interestingly, Jesus made sure the man understood that if he followed Jesus, he wouldn't have a place to call home. Jesus emphasized the sacrifice associated with being his disciple.

The second man also seemed interested, but wanted to attend to some family business. In reply, Jesus forbade the man from attending his father's funeral, which seems quite harsh. However, it is unlikely that the man's father was already dead. The man was probably asking to go home and wait for his father to die so that he could get his inheritance and then follow Jesus without having to worry about money. Jesus explained that discipleship does not work that way. You either leave everything and follow or you don't follow at all. Jesus summed up the teaching of this section very clearly in Luke 14:33: "Any of you who does not give up everything he has cannot be my disciple."

The call of Jesus is to take up your cross and lose your life (Mark 8:34). German theologian Dietrich Bonhoeffer wrote, "When God calls a man, he bids him come and die."[12] By this he meant that a man has to give up everything he holds dear and submit his entire self to the will of God. Bonhoeffer was talking about the spiritual, intellectual and emotional dimension of life, to be sure, but he also meant the physical. We are to love God to the point of not shrinking back even from physical death in the course of following God's call.

Bonhoeffer was not mouthing empty platitudes. He understood the call to death in every sense of the word. An outspoken critic of the Nazis during World War II, Bonhoeffer had plenty of opportunity to safely wait out the war working as an academic in America. However, he decided that God wanted him back in Germany, working with the resistance movement to free his homeland. After being arrested for taking part in an unsuccessful attempt on Hitler's life, Bonhoeffer was hanged in Flossenburg concentration camp on April 9, 1945, just three weeks before it was liberated by the Allies.

The Bible agrees that the call of Christ is a call to die, sometimes even physically. Look at the radical commission Jesus gave Peter. After being asked three times whether he loved Jesus, "Peter was hurt because Jesus asked him the third time, 'Do you love me?' He said, 'Lord, you know all things; you know that I love you.

Jesus said, "Feed my sheep. I tell you the truth, when you were younger you dressed yourself and went where you wanted; but when you are old you will stretch out your hands, and someone else will dress you and lead you where you do not want to go." Jesus said this to indicate the kind of death by which Peter would glorify God. Then he said to him, "Follow me!" (John 21:15-19)

Three times Jesus asked Peter if he loved Christ more than anything else in the world, and three times Peter was told to work at his pastoral calling. Then the kicker: Jesus told Peter explicitly that this calling is going to lead directly to Peter's death! The cost of discipleship doesn't get any more expensive than that.

The writer of Hebrews describes the heroes of the faith this way:

Some faced jeers and flogging, while still others were chained and put in prison. They were stoned; they were sawed in two; they were put to death by the sword. They went about in sheepskins and goatskins, destitute, persecuted and mistreated – the world was not worthy of them. They wandered in deserts and mountains, and in caves and holes in the ground. These were all commended for their faith, yet none of them received what had been promised. God had planned something better for us so that only together with us would they be made perfect. (Hebrews 11:36-40)

What should we do to emulate these brave souls? Notice the race terminology in the conclusion of the passage:

Therefore, since we are surrounded by such a great cloud of witnesses, let us throw off everything that hinders and the sin that so easily entangles, and let us run with perseverance the race marked out for us. Let us fix our eyes on Jesus, the author and perfecter of our faith, who for the joy set before him endured the cross, scorning its shame, and sat down at the right hand of the throne of God. Consider him who endured such opposition from sinful men, so that you will not grow weary and lose heart. In your struggle against sin, you have not yet resisted to the point of shedding your blood. (Hebrews 12:1-4)

Isn't that amazing? One of the points of this passage is that those who are struggling along the narrow road should take heart because, after all, they haven't had to follow the great heroes of the faith and die! At least not yet! They "have not yet resisted to the point" of death. The implication is clear – they might have to do just that.

Of course, as we also see in this passage, the greatest example of self-denial and radical faith was Jesus himself. His submission to the will of the Father was absolute. When faced with nothing less than excruciating torture and death on a cross, Jesus submitted to the will of the Father in the Garden of Gethsemane: "My Father, if it is possible, may this cup be taken from me. Yet not as I will, but as you will" (Matthew 26:39). This is to be our approach to discipleship as well. Our prayer should be "Not my will but yours be done, Father, even if it means death." In other words, we are to sacrifice whatever is necessary, even if it means out own life:

Your attitude should be the same as that of Christ Jesus: Who, being in very nature God, did not consider equality with God something to be grasped, but made himself nothing, taking the very nature of a servant, being made in human likeness. And being found in appearance as a man, he humbled himself and became obedient to death – even death on a cross! (Phil. 2:5-8)

That is real sacrifice. It is also true love.

The Benefits Outweigh the Cost
Sacrifice is difficult, but I don't want to let the message of this chapter leave you feeling discouraged. As such, let's conclude on a high note: the benefits of sacrifice far outweigh the cost! Although sacrifice hurts – if it didn't it wouldn't be sacrifice – it is immensely rewarding eventually. At the end of the day, you see what a fool you would have been to hold on to what you had to sacrifice, because what you get is so much better. It is always worth it. Many happy years of marriage with your wife is better than any basketball game. Selling everything else you own to get the piece of land that has the treasure is always a good deal (Matthew 13:44). When I think back to leaving Canada and giving up the job and the car and the coat, compared to what I have gained, it's no contest. My life has been awesome and I have no doubt that I would have missed out on a huge amount of blessings if I had held on to everything I loved back then.

The principle that God exalts those who humble themselves before him in sacrifice is a major theme in scripture. The best picture of it, of course, is Jesus himself. We previously quoted Philippians 2 in discussing how Jesus humbled himself in becoming a man. Look at how that passage concludes: "Therefore

God exalted him to the highest place and gave him the name that is above every name, that at the name of Jesus every knee should bow, in heaven and on earth and under the earth, and every tongue acknowledge that Jesus Christ is Lord, to the glory of God the Father" (Philippians 2:9-11). The reward for his obedience was far greater than the sacrifice.

The episode with the rich young ruler teaches a similar lesson. After the man refused to sacrifice him money, Jesus explained "How hard it is for the rich to enter the kingdom of God! Indeed, it is easier for a camel to go through the eye of a needle than for a rich man to enter the kingdom of God" (Luke 18:24-25). The disciples were astonished at this and Peter, perhaps wanting to confirm that he was not on the same track as the young ruler, blurted out "We have left all to follow you!" (Luke 18:28). Jesus reassured him: "I tell you the truth, no one who has left home or wife or brothers or parents or children for the sake of the kingdom of God will fail to receive many times as much in this age and, in the age to come, eternal life" (Luke 18:29-30). The disciples had sacrificed, but they would gain far more in the long run.

God's plan for us is to live with him in the Promised Land. This is far superior to worshiping idols as a slave in Egypt, so it is always the right move to leave the idols of Egypt behind. As Jim Elliot, a missionary who was martyred attempting to bring the gospel to South American tribes, wrote, "He is no fool who gives what he cannot keep to gain that which he cannot lose."[13]

Chapter 3

Testing God

Back to Canada

At the beginning of the last chapter I told you about a dilemma I faced as a young adult about whether or not to move to California. Well, I did end up going and for six months, everything was amazing. It was one of those experiences that, when you think back on it, you honestly can't remember any drawbacks. I loved everything about my new life: my classes, the kids I was working with, the friends I was making, and the San Francisco Bay Area. To top it off, I felt like my relationship with God was strong and getting even better. I could see him doing miracles around me all the time, I could sense his closeness to me, and I was excited to tell others about him. It just was a great time to be alive.

Then it all came to a screeching halt. Basically, I ran out of money. I simply didn't have the funds to register for a new semester of classes and had to return to Canada. I was shocked and confused.

I had spent the previous summer working at a camp for inner city kids. It didn't pay well but I had been sure that the money for school would come from somewhere. After all, I had seen God provide for me in supernatural ways for the past six months. He had worked out my living situation and provided food and a job for me. Not to mention that he had been doing so many wonderful things in my spiritual life and had been using me to reach others. Why would God pull the rug out from under me now? I had no idea.

The next few months were tough. I worked and read and pined for California. It seemed like my life was at a standstill. Slowly, however, the disillusionment gave way to a renewed and deeper trust in God. I began to realize that God still had things under control and that he was busy molding and shaping me. I started to see areas in my life in which I needed to grow and I took steps to address them. When I went back to California the following year, it was with a better attitude and a more mature faith. My time in exile had been very good for me.

We will discuss the specific lesson I learned later in this chapter, but for now let me point out that sending people out into the wilderness, literally and figuratively, is very consistent with God's pattern in history. God does not just ask us to sacrifice stuff; sometimes he simply takes it away (or takes us away from it.)

The Israelites Test God; Jesus Doesn't
To recap the previous chapter briefly, God asks us to sacrifice in order to 1. Show us whom or what we are loving 2. Move us toward loving God. In other words, the demand for sacrifice is intended to test and to humble. Well, rather than always ask for sacrifice, sometimes God tests and humbles us by simply throwing us into a situation in which we experience loss. Sometime he sends us to the desert.

This is what he did to the Israelites. He took them from the Red Sea directly into the Desert of Shur, where within a few days they were complaining about a lack of water. (Exo. 15:22-24). Why didn't he find a nicer route or send a few nicely equipped air conditioned coaches? Because he wanted to test and humble them: "Remember how the LORD your God led you all the way in the desert these forty years, to humble you and to test you in order to know what was in your heart, whether or not you would keep his commands" (Deut. 8:2).

Unfortunately, many of the Israelites did not respond well to desert conditions. I wish it wasn't the case, but I can definitely relate to these Israelites. Imagine it: they had just seen God defeat the armies and gods of Egypt and set them free. They must have been on an incredible emotional high after the Red Sea. And then: desert. Hot, dry, dusty wilderness. It had to be a shock. I can imagine them thinking, "Why would the God who has done such mighty things for us allow us to experience this misery? I know he has the power to change this, so why doesn't he?"

The main problem here, it seems, is that the people had started to have too high a view of themselves. They had developed the notion that, as the people God had called to himself and brought out of Egypt, they must have some special value that warranted this effort. They had become proud and needed to be humbled. The reason I interpret this passage in this manner is the way Jesus referenced this episode when he was sent to the wilderness.

Like the Israelites, immediately after being baptized, Jesus went out in the desert to be tested. Jesus was tempted three times by Satan. In the second episode,

> The devil took [Jesus] to the holy city and had him stand on the highest point of the temple. "If you are the Son of God," he said, "throw yourself down. For it is written: 'He will command his angels concerning you, and they will lift you up in their hands, so that you will not strike your foot against a stone.'"

> Jesus answered him, "It is also written: 'Do not put the Lord your God to the test.'"(Matt. 4:5-7)

Satan tried to get Jesus to demand a miracle from God. Jesus rightly refused and supported his decision by quoting Deuteronomy 6:16: "Do not test the LORD your God as you did at Massah." This is a reference to the incident we are discussing: the one in which the Israelites grumbled about their lack of water. When they confronted Moses, he replied, "Why do you quarrel with me? Why do you put the LORD to the test?" (Exodus 17:2). That episode concludes with Moses inquiring of the Lord, who told him to strike a rock with his staff to bring water out. "So Moses did this in the sight of the elders of Israel. And he called the place Massah and Meribah because the Israelites quarreled and because they tested the LORD saying, 'Is the LORD among us or not?'" (Exodus 17:6-7).

The Wrong Focus

The key to understanding this story (and why Jesus refers to it) is the question, "Is the LORD among us or not?" I think that perhaps the word "us" should be in italics. The focus of the sentence is the Israelites, not God. That is the problem.

The Israelites were thirsty and appealed to God (through Moses) to do a miracle for them. But notice the nature of this appeal. In asking if the LORD was among them, they were not questioning the existence of God or even whether or not he had the power to provide water. They were not asking, "Can God do this?" They were asking, "Are we special people or not? Are we God's chosen family or not? Is he among us in a unique way or not?" It was a rhetorical question meant to force God's hand. What they were saying in statement form is "We are special people. We deserve to have you do what we want. Where is our water!?"

The Israelites knew God existed and that he had power to provide water – they had just seen the plagues and the parting of the Red Sea and the miraculous provision of manna. When they complained about water, they were not questioning his power; they were telling God that they deserved to have him use that power on their behalf.

The way they reacted to being thirsty showed that the Israelites still had a lot to learn about God's motives and their own place in his plan. They let their pride rise up even in the midst of being plucked out of slavery through no power of their own. They thought that somehow they were worthy to be saved and have their thirst quenched as well.

While I was in Canada wishing to be back in California, I realized that I had started to think this way as well. While ostensibly I was focused on doing the Lord's work and knowing him better, in reality I was focused on taking classes that *I* enjoyed and doing work that *I* found meaningful and living in a place that *I* found exhilarating. It was all about me. When God took me out of that situation I couldn't figure out why he wouldn't provide the money for me to keep going to school. Hadn't I exhibited great faith in moving? Wouldn't it be better for me to keep studying the Bible and working with kids so I could lead more to him? Wasn't I special? My questions revealed that my focus was on myself rather than God. I was acting as if God needed me to be on his team; as if I was deserving of his work. He doesn't and I'm not. I was proud and needed to be humbled. God revealed that by sending me to the wilderness.

Jesus was not proud. This too was revealed in the desert. Satan tried to get Jesus to focus on himself ("If you are the Son of God...") and test God in the same way as the Israelites and I did, but he would not. In the same way that the Israelites said "We are special. Quench our thirst!" and I said "I am special. Pay for my school!" Satan wanted Jesus to say to the Father "I am special. Catch me when I fall!" Jesus would not do that because he was focused on the Father's glory, not his own. This is what the Israelites should have been concentrating on as well, as should have I. Rather than always thinking about what God has taken away from us and should do for us, we should be thinking of how God is going to be glorified in and through us. To test God is to try to get him to do something for our glory rather than his.

God's Reason for Everything

One of the main lessons of the wilderness is that we are dependent creatures. The desert is a place where man cannot survive without help. In the wilderness the Israelites needed God to feed and clothe them and fight their battles. So do we. As a corollary to this truth is the fact that God takes care of us for his own glory, not for ours. If we ever start to treat God as if we are deserving of his care or that he is bound to take care of us for our own sake, we've missed the point of God's plan.

Unfortunately, that sentiment is quite common today. We speak of God as if he'd be lost without us. I read a children's devotional recently that insinuated that God created us because he was lonely. That simply isn't the case. God did not need to create the universe or us. He was not lonely or incomplete. He was and is completely satisfied and content; indeed he delights and has always delighted in simply being God. Creation resulted from a bubbling over of this delight. God's joy overflowed like a fountain in creation and everything that resulted is intended to glorify him. "The heavens declare the glory of God; the skies proclaim the work of his hands" (Psalm 19:1). Why do they do this? Because that is what they were created to do. God's glory is revealed through his creation. Paul explains in Romans "For since the creation of the world God's invisible qualities – his eternal power and divine nature – have been clearly seen, being understood from what has been made" (Romans 1:20). God's intention in creating the universe was to show his greatness. Man is the most explicit demonstration of that greatness. The creation account in Genesis reaches its high point with Adam and Eve because they are made in the very image of God (Gen. 1:26) and therefore glorify him the most. "Bring my sons from afar and my daughters from the ends of the earth – everyone who is called by my name, whom I created for my glory, whom I formed and made" (Isa. 43:6b-7).

The Glory of God in Redemption
God's "passion for his glory"[14] motivated the original creation and can also clearly be seen in the redemption of that creation. The Exodus is a prime example of that. Scripture is clear that God released the Israelites from bondage and remained faithful to them through the wilderness because of his passion for his glory. For example, God explained to Moses that he would take the Israelites to the Red Sea rather that a shorter route so that he could bring glory to himself through one more tremendous miracle: "I will gain glory for myself through Pharaoh and all his army, and the Egyptians will know that I am the LORD" (Exodus 14:4).

In future years the Israelites would look back at the Exodus and recall what had happened and why. Isaiah wrote that "his people remembered the days of old" and asked,

Where is he...who sent his glorious arm of power to be at Moses' right hand, who divided the waters before them, to gain for himself everlasting renown, who led them through the depths? Like a horse in open country, they did not stumble; like cattle that go down to the plain, they were given rest by the Spirit of the Lord. This is how you guided your people to make for yourself a glorious name. (Isaiah 63:12-14)

When David was called to build a temple for God, he responded with appropriate understanding of God's motivation, describing Israel as the "the one nation on earth that God went out to redeem as a people for himself, and to make a name for himself, and to perform great and awesome wonders by driving out nations and their gods from before your people, whom you redeemed from Egypt?" (2 Sam. 7:23).

Later, when Israel rebelled against God, he explained clearly why he was still intent on redeeming them. It was not because they deserved it:

And wherever they went among the nations they profaned my holy name, for it was said of them, "These are the LORD's people, and yet they had to leave his land." I had concern for my holy name, which the house of Israel profaned among the nations where they had gone.

Therefore say to the house of Israel, "This is what the Sovereign LORD says: It is not for your sake, O house of Israel, that I am going to do these things, but for the sake of my holy name, which you have profaned among the nations where you have gone. I will show the holiness of my great name, which has been profaned among the nations, the name you have profaned among them. Then the nations will know that I am the LORD, declares the Sovereign LORD, when I show myself holy through you before their eyes.

"For I will take you out of the nations; I will gather you from all the countries and bring you back into your own land. ... I want you to know that I am not doing this for your sake, declares the Sovereign LORD. Be ashamed and disgraced for your conduct, O house of Israel!" (Ezekiel 36:20-24, 32)

God sums up the motivation for his faithfulness and mercy nicely in Isaiah 48: "For my own name's sake I delay my wrath; for the sake of my praise I hold it back from you, so as not to cut you off. See, I have refined you, though not as silver; I have tested you in the furnace of affliction. For my own sake, for my own sake, I do this. How can I let myself be defamed? I will not yield my glory to another" (Isaiah 48:9-11).

Just as God's passion for his glory is what motivated him to redeem and stay faithful to the Israelites, it also motivates him to redeem and remain faithful to us. God saves us because he is glorified in saving us, just as Paul explained to the Ephesians: "In him we were also chosen, having been predestined according to the plan of him who works out everything in conformity with the purpose of his will, in order that we, who were the first to hope in Christ, might be for the praise of his glory" (Eph. 1:13).

Our Value and God's Glory

Does God think we are valuable? Of course. But we shouldn't interpret that through the prism of our culture's cult of self-esteem. God did not wander though Wal-Mart one day, happen to see me down the aisle, and suddenly realize he had found the most ravishing and valuable creature in the universe. He made me. I have value according to the worth he gave me at creation.

This happens to be very, very high, since humans are made in his image (Genesis 1:27), but my value is especially high because I can glorify him more than, say, sheep and birds (Matthew 6:26, 10:31, 12:12). According to John Piper,

> The love of God for sinners is not his making much of them, but his graciously freeing and empowering them to enjoy making much of him.
>
> As [Jonathan] Edwards says, "God is their good." Therefore, if God would do us good, he must direct us to his worth, not ours....Today, people typically feel loved if you make much of them and help them feel valued. The bottom line in their happiness is that they are made much of.
>
> Edwards observes, with stunning modern relevance, "True saints have their minds, in the first place, inexpressibly pleased and delighted with ... the things of God. But the dependence of the affections of hypocrites is in a contrary order: they first rejoice ... that they are made so much of by God; and then on that ground, he seems in a sort, lovely to them."[15] [16]

As Piper points out, the fact that God's love for us is not primarily about our value should keep us from loving immaturely. By that I mean that we should not love God only because he values us or even because he does nice things for us. We should love him because of who he is.

My wife Kendra and I have four children. Our major challenge as parents (as all parents can testify) is to try to make our children understand that they are not the center of the universe and that their parents do not exist to grant their every desire. To not attempt this would be to spoil our children and hinder our relationship with them. For example, if I were to ask my youngest to describe why she likes her daddy, I am quite sure her answer would center on all the things that I do for her. "My daddy plays with me, feeds me, reads books to me, changes me and gets me dressed," etc. Hopefully this will change over time, and as she gets older my daughter will be able to answer somewhat more objectively; "My daddy plays with me and reads to me and he tells people about Jesus and writes neat books," etc.

We need the same maturation process in our relationship with God. We need to develop a love for him that is based on more than the fact that "He thinks I am special." We don't want to treat God like one of those early grade school romances. You don't know a certain person exists until one day you find out that they like you. All of a sudden your opinion of them goes way up. As we all should know by now, that is no way to pursue a relationship. If you don't like someone for who they are, rather than what they think of you, you're in trouble.

Is God an Egomaniac?

When presented with this argument, some people have told me that I make it sound like God is overcome by pride and just needs to get over himself. Is this the case? Of course not. The reason this cannot be so is that God could never put undo focus on himself. On the other hand, we can certainly put undo focus on ourselves. God is worthy of all the focus and praise he can get; we are not.

The reason pride is wrong for us is that we are not deserving to receive glory. Pride used to be referred to as "vain-glory," and I think that term does an excellent job of describing the problem. Pride is glory that is given in vain. It is glory that should not be given because the object of the glory is not glorious. We should not focus on and praise ourselves because we are not worthy to be focused on and praised. However, God is. He is worthy of all glory and honor and therefore can never be guilty of vain-glory.

God is the only independent one. Everything else and everyone else is dependent on him. It is fine for God to consider himself the center of all because he is the center of all. It is fine for God to accept worship (worship means to have worth ascribed) because he is worthy. God is above all. He is the most valuable entity there is. It is not alright for me to accept that same worship because I am not. For me to ascribe worth to something that is not worthy is foolishness.

For example, we ascribe different amounts of worth to different things. Gold has a certain amount of value, and silver has another. We generally agree that gold is more valuable than silver, and we would think it foolish for someone to worship silver to such an extent that he would trade two ounces of gold for an ounce of silver. To do so would be to practice vain-glory. Now you might say that precious metals are valued somewhat subjectively, and you wouldn't judge too harshly if someone happened to like silver better than gold. Fair enough. But what about this situation? Suppose a person valued silver more than his relationship to his wife? Or the life of his child? What if a man was willing to trade his son or daughter into slavery for a few ounces of metal? I hope that we find this situation easier to judge, as it is very objective. This would simply be wrong. The life of a child and one's relationship with a spouse is much more valuable than any amount of money. To worship money over family is to reverse the established order of the universe and should be condemned.

This is why God is so adamant that he will not give his glory to another. To do so is to reverse the order of the universe, and not even God can do that. For God to not take the glory for himself or to delight fully in anything or anyone but himself would be idolatry in the very same way as to ascribe worth to money over people. When God works for his own glory, when he asks for worship and forbids the worship of anything else, he is simply keeping the universe in proper order. When we reject this order by worshiping and serving the created thing rather than the creator, we bring all sorts of trouble on ourselves (Romans 1:18-25).

Testing God and Passing God's Test
In the wilderness God reveals whether we are living for God's glory or our own. Our goal is to pass God's test by not testing God. We want to be like Jesus rather than me or the Israelites. Thankfully, though, even if we fail the test at first, the wilderness experience is designed to allow you to learn from your failures. The desert shows you who you love, but it also pushes you to love properly. God's tests are not just pass/fail. Even if we fail at first, the act of going through the test should actually help us change our lives for the better and ultimately be able to pass the test. Here is how it works.

When God takes us into the wilderness, not only is he testing us to expose whether or not we are going to complain, but he is teaching us that we have no reason to complain, because everything else is unworthy of our worship anyway. We should find our joy, contentment, and sustenance from God, not from the thing/place/person we are missing. When we survive and even thrive in the wilderness, we should see the futility of trusting in that thing and therefore not complain. This is something we probably would not have known if it had never been taken away.

When God took the Israelites into a place without food and water, he was testing them to see how they would react, but he was also trying to teach them that "man does not live on bread alone but on every word that comes from the mouth of the LORD." He intended to break down their worship of themselves and their stuff by taking that stuff away and showing them that they didn't need it.

While I was in Canada, not only did I realize that God didn't need me in California; I started to see that I didn't need California. I renewed my commitment to doing whatever God wanted for his sake alone.

Interestingly, this is far from the only time God has used this pattern with me. In fact, the only reason I was even in a position of wanting to serve God at all at this point was because he had already put me through several testing episodes in the year and a half prior. (Insert your own comment about the level of pride I must have started with here.)

For example, as a 21 year old, I was the epitome of foolish self-confidence. I really felt like I had life by the tail and could do whatever I wanted with it. That ended one cold spring night on the Canadian plains. My good friend and I were driving home from playing hockey in southern Saskatchewan when we crossed a bridge covered in "black" (extremely transparent) ice. My short-box pickup truck skidded out of control and flipped over several times. I was thrown through the driver's side window. The next thing I remember is waking up in a hospital bed, unable to move.

The brush with death had a clarifying effect on me. As I lay paralyzed, I realized that I had been arrogant and foolish and that all I had been chasing after in life – money, stuff, fun experiences – was a complete waste of time. At that moment, all I wanted to do was get right with God, so I repented of my stupidity and misplaced faith and surrendered my life to his service.

God humbled me by taking away my health (at least briefly – I had no major injuries and was walking the next day), my truck, and almost my life. He put me through a test and, although I was not putting my faith in him as I entered the test, by the end I was. The act of going through the test had helped me pass it.

One of the consequences of that night was that I spent my first summer working at that camp for inner city kids I already mentioned. As a farm boy, this was a bit out of my comfort zone. However, I went in with confidence that I had the strength to do it. That was a big mistake.

The camp ran for nine weeks and by week six and seven most of the workers were exhausted and longing to be done. I, however, still felt good and was starting to look down at the "weaklings" I was working with. Then, in week eight, I received what I am sure is still considered to be the worst cabin of boys in the history of Camp May Mac. These guys were the toughest, brattiest kids I had ever met, and I had eight of them. It was simply too much. One day while walking down to the dining hall, I finally snapped. It is not that anything especially bad or out of the ordinary happened – just one more vulgar comment about me and my mother, as far as I remember – but it was the last straw. I grabbed one of the boys by the shirt and lifted him off the ground. His eyes got really big, and I could see that he felt I might really harm him. Then it hit me: *I* felt I might really harm him. I quickly dropped him to the ground, handed my group off to another counselor, and went into the woods. There I literally cried out to God, "I can't do this."

"Exactly," was God's response. "It is about time you understood that. You *can't* do this, at least not in your own strength. Trusting in yourself is going to get you nowhere. Put your faith in me."

Tough circumstances are designed not only to test us, but to humble us and enable us to come out of the test with a passing grade. I had become proud, and God had to put me in a situation that would humble me.

Before leaving this subject, I want to point out that testing will not always bring humility. Although my testing experiences resulted in repentance, it is conceivable that my heart could have hardened instead. I could have got angry at God for not paying my college bill or allowing my car accident or giving me such hard campers. I am sure we all know people who harbor a grudge against God for some harm they think he has caused them in the past. Traveling through the wilderness can result in hard hearts as well as soft, as we will see in later chapters. Paul contrasts "godly sorrow," which leads to repentance and "worldly sorrow," which does not (2 Corinthians 7:9-11). The correct response to a test is humility, not greater pride. Indeed, rather than becoming angry, we can actually rejoice in our trials, as Paul exemplifies and James teaches:

> To keep me from becoming conceited because of these surpassingly great revelations, there was given me a thorn in my flesh, a messenger of Satan, to torment me. Three times I pleaded with the Lord to take it away from me. But he said to me, "My grace is sufficient for you, for my power is made perfect in weakness." Therefore I will boast all the more gladly about my weaknesses, so that Christ's power may rest on me. That is why, for Christ's sake, I delight in weaknesses, in insults, in hardships, in persecutions, in

difficulties. For when I am weak, then I am strong. (2 Cor. 12:7-10)

"Consider it pure joy, my brothers, whenever you face trials of many kinds, because you know that the testing of your faith develops perseverance. Perseverance must finish its work so that you may be mature and complete, not lacking anything" (Jam. 1:2-4).

Chapter 4

The Body and Blood of Christ

Passover

If I had to point to one thing that God has tried to teach me over the years, it is that I need God to make it through. I can't do it on my own. God must be my strength, he must be my sustenance; he must provide my ultimate salvation. Sounds nice in theory, right, but how does that work in practice? How exactly do I get strength and sustenance from God? In other words, how does he supply it and how do I obtain it? This is something I have continually struggled with in my Christian life, and frankly, am still working through. However, again, I think the Exodus story provides some good insight as to God's model for providing for his people on their journey home.

To start this chapter, I would like to back up in the Exodus story to the tenth and final plague on Egypt. Even after all the suffering his kingdom had faced in the first nine plagues, Pharaoh still would not let the Hebrews go (Exodus 10:27), so Moses explained that there would be one more act: God was going to kill all the firstborn of Egypt (Exodus 11).

You might wonder why God had to go to such lengths. After all, isn't killing all the firstborn in the land a little harsh, even for someone as stubborn as the Pharaoh? Here it is important to remember that the plagues were acts of judgment. God used the plagues to punish Egypt for its rebellion against him and worship of other gods. (Exodus 6:6; 12:12).

God is just in dealing with nations. Rebellious people reap what they sow (Psalm 9:15-20) and the wages of sin is death (Romans 6:23). Through the death of the firstborn, God was bringing justice on Egypt for their sins. But what about the sins of the rest of the people? Why just the firstborn? And what about the sins of Israel? Were they any different in their rejection of God? No. This is where the symbolic and allegorical nature of the Exodus story really comes into play.

I find two aspects of the final plague very interesting.

First, God limited the punishment to the firstborn. Though they are not the only ones that are guilty, the firstborn of every family pays the penalty for everyone else. God would have been justified in simply wiping out the entire population, but limited the punishment to a representative group.

Second, God gave a way for even that group to escape his wrath. He offered the people the option of having their punishment placed on a lamb. Rather than the firstborn of a family paying the price for everyone, a young sheep would die in his place. God explained to Moses that each family was to take a lamb and slaughter it at twilight. Then they were to put the blood on the sides and tops of the doorframes of the houses and eat the lambs.

> "On that same night I will pass through Egypt and strike down every firstborn – both men and animals – and I will bring judgment on all the gods of Egypt. I am the LORD. The blood will be a sign for you on the houses where you are; and when I see the blood, I will pass over you. No destructive plague will touch you when I strike Egypt." (Exodus 12:12-13)

By placing the blood on the doorframe, those that followed God's plan escaped judgment. Sin still resulted in death, but rather than everyone's death, or even the death of the firstborn, the penalty for this group's sin was paid by the death of a lamb.

Jesus the Lamb

So the way out of Egypt went directly under the blood of the lamb. The way to obtain God's grace was to follow the directions for the Passover. Only those who did so escaped God's wrath and were set free from slavery.

In exactly the same fashion, the way to our Promised Land goes directly under the blood of the lamb. Of course for us the lamb is Jesus. He is the one who takes our punishment upon himself. He is the firstborn of God, the pure and spotless one who took the wrath of God when he died on the cross. Because of Jesus we are able to escape Satan's clutches.

The connection between Jesus and the Passover lamb is abundantly clear in scripture. For example, John the Baptist's first words when he saw Jesus were, "Look, the Lamb of God, who takes away the sin of the world!" (John 1:29), a reference he used the next day as well (John 1:36). Paul explicitly calls Christ "our Passover lamb" (1 Corinthians 5:7), and Peter explains why we should live holy lives: "For you know that it was not with perishable things such as silver or gold that you were redeemed from the empty way of life handed down to you from your forefathers, but with the precious blood of Christ, a lamb without blemish or defect" (1 Peter 1:18-19). In addition, the book of Revelation has several references to Jesus being the lamb, including 7:9, 12:11, 13:8, 14:1, 15:3, 17:14, 19:9 and 21:22.

Jesus' connection with the Passover lamb becomes even clearer when we examine the story of his passion. As part of his instructions to Moses, God commanded the Israelites to commemorate the Passover with a week-long festival every year. It is no coincidence that Jesus' death occurred exactly during this Passover celebration. As the people remembered and celebrated the lamb that was slain for the slaves in Egypt, the fulfillment of that lamb was slain for them and us. Here are some of the interesting scriptural parallels that make this connection clear.

The fifth day before Passover was lamb selection day, when the families would go and choose a lamb to sacrifice on Passover (the 10th of the month in Exodus 12:3, Passover occurred on the 14th). This is the exact day that Jesus entered Jerusalem during Passion Week, the Lamb of God chosen before the foundation of the world (John 12:12-13, Revelation 13:8).

The Passover lamb had to be without defect, pure and spotless (Exodus 12:5). Jesus lived a perfect life; he was sinless and pure (1 Peter 1:19). "He committed no sin, and no deceit was found in his mouth" (1 Peter 2:22). According to Paul, "God made him who had no sin to be sin for us, so that in him we might become the righteousness of God" (2 Corinthians 5:21).

During the first Passover, the blood was applied to the doorposts using hyssop, a Mediterranean plant. Hyssop is never mentioned in the Bible outside of the context of purification and forgiveness of sins, and the image of a man lifting a hyssop plant into the air towards a bloody piece of wood would certainly remind a Jew of the Passover. That is exactly what happened in the moment before Jesus' death. A sponge was attached to a hyssop plant, dipped in wine-vinegar, and offered to Jesus (John 19:29).

On the day of the Passover celebration a priest would blow his horn at 3:00 p.m., the moment the Passover lamb was sacrificed. At the sounding of the horn, all the people would pause and contemplate the death of the lamb for their sins. It was at this very moment on Good Friday that Jesus cried out, "It is finished" and gave up his spirit. (Matthew 27:45-50; Mark 15:33-37; Luke 23:44-46; John 19:30).

The Passover lamb was to have none of its bones broken (Exodus 12:46). It was common during crucifixions to break the legs of the victim in order to hasten death. The only way for a person to breathe while hanging on a cross is to push up with their legs, so if the legs are broken, death by asphyxiation comes quickly. During Jesus' crucifixion, soldiers broke the legs of the two men next to Jesus but did not need to do the same to Jesus, as he was already dead (John 19:31-34). John makes the connection between Jesus and the Old Testament clear by pointing out that this was a fulfillment of prophecy (John 19:35).

All of these "coincidences" are meant to show us that Jesus was our Passover lamb. We deserve to die for our sin, but instead of making us take the punishment ourselves or place it on our firstborn, Jesus took it all. His death allowed us to be set free.

So how do we appropriate that grace? What does it mean for us to follow the directions of the Passover? First, when we acknowledge our need for a savior and repenting of our rebellion against God, we spiritually place his blood on the doorposts of our heart and are covered by the blood of the lamb. This is the part of salvation that I focused on in my youth and it certainly is a major part.

As I mentioned in Chapter One, I considered salvation to consist entirely of God looking my direction and seeing only the blood of Jesus. This finds a parallel in the Passover in that, as God looked over Egypt, there is a sense in which he either saw a sinner or the blood of the lamb that was covering a sinner. Those that were covered by the blood of the Passover lamb were saved and those that are covered by the blood of Jesus are saved.

However, that is not the whole story. In fact, the directions for the Passover actually include very little about the act of putting the blood on the doorposts. However, God does spend a lot of time giving directions about how the people should eat the lamb. Indeed, I think you can see that the focus of the Passover instructions is the eating:

> The LORD said to Moses and Aaron in Egypt, "This month is to be for you the first month, the first month of your year. Tell the whole community of Israel that on the tenth day of this month each man is to take a lamb for his family, one for each household. If any household is too small for a whole lamb, they must share one with their nearest neighbor, having taken into account the number of people there are. You are to determine the amount of lamb needed in accordance with what each person will eat. The animals you choose must be year-old males without defect, and you may take them from the sheep or the goats. Take care of them until the fourteenth day of the month, when all the people of the community of Israel must slaughter them at twilight. Then they are to take some of the blood and put it on the sides and tops of the doorframes of the houses where they eat the lambs. That same night they are to eat the meat roasted over the fire, along with bitter herbs, and bread made without yeast. Do not eat the meat raw or cooked in water, but roast it over the fire – head, legs and inner parts. Do not leave any of it till morning; if some is left till morning, you must burn it. This is how you are to eat it: with your cloak tucked into your belt, your sandals on your feet and your staff in

your hand. Eat it in haste; it is the LORD's Passover. (Exodus 12:1-11)

The Israelites didn't just have to place the blood of the lamb on the door. They had to *eat* the lamb. Before my concentrated study of Exodus, I had never really noticed that. I always just kind of assumed that the blood on the door and the blood on the cross was basically the whole story. But the Passover was not just about covering the Israelites with the blood of the lamb. It was also about nourishing them with the body of the lamb. They received grace in the form of forgiveness from the lamb's blood, but they also received grace in the form of sustenance and strength from the lamb's body. Then, as they traveled across the desert, God continued to sustain them by providing water and manna from Heaven (Exodus 16 and 17). So to get to the Promised Land, they had to partake of the lamb, the water from the rock and the manna from heaven.

All of these things were types of Christ! Jesus is our Passover lamb; Jesus is our water from the rock; Jesus is our manna from heaven. In the same way the Israelites partook of the lamb, water, and manna, we are to partake of Jesus. That is how we are strengthened and sustained on the journey.

The writers of the New Testament were very clear that the elements that strengthened and sustained the Israelites are representative of Jesus, and Jesus himself was very clear that we are to partake of him.

For example, consider John Chapter 6. Jesus miraculously feeds 5000 people and then sets off to be alone. However, the crowds, eager for more food, find him on the other side of the lake (John 6:24). He tells them that they should concentrate less on trying to find material bread that will spoil and more on searching out spiritual bread, which will get them eternal life (John

6:25-26). Here Jesus is already insinuating that he is the one who can supply them that bread, but the people seem to be unsure of what that meant. They ask Jesus to give them a sign similar to what Moses did in calling down manna from Heaven (John 6:30-31). Jesus replies that it was not Moses who provided bread, but God, and now, Jesus continues, God is providing spiritual bread from Heaven that will give eternal life. The people ask for that bread and Jesus answers "I am the bread of life. He who comes to me will never go hungry, and he who believes in me will never go thirsty" (John 6:35)

Jesus told the people that the manna in the wilderness was just a foreshadowing of the ultimate manna from Heaven: Jesus! Jesus is the fulfillment the physical food that God provided in the wilderness. Just as the Israelites ate the manna in the wilderness to sustain them on the journey, we must partake of Jesus. The difference is the manna was physical bread that decayed, while Jesus is spiritual bread that does not. Jesus made all this clear as he continued the teaching:

> I am the bread that came down from heaven…I tell you the truth, he who believes has everlasting life. I am the bread of life. Your forefathers ate the manna in the desert, yet they died. But here is the bread that comes down from heaven, which a man may eat and not die. I am the living bread that came down from heaven. If anyone eats of this bread, he will live forever. This bread is my flesh, which I will give for the life of the world. (John 6:41; 47-51)

The Jews were confused about this teaching, so Jesus continued to clarify:

I tell you the truth, unless you eat the flesh of the Son of Man and drink his blood, you have no life in you. Whoever eats my flesh and drinks my blood has eternal life, and I will raise him up at the last day. For my flesh is real food and my blood is real drink. Whoever eats my flesh and drinks my blood remains in me, and I in him. Just as the living Father sent me and I live because of the Father, so the one who feeds on me will live because of me. This is the bread that came down from heaven. Your forefathers ate manna and died, but he who feeds on this bread will live forever. (John 6:53-58)

The teaching is clear: if we are to make it across the wilderness, we must not only start the journey under the blood of Jesus, but we must continually partake of the body of Jesus. He is our manna.

He is also our water from the rock. In 1 Corinthians 10:2-4, Paul explains that the Israelites "were all baptized into Moses in the cloud and in the sea. They ate the same spiritual food and drank the same spiritual drink; for they drank from the spiritual rock that accompanied them, and that rock was Christ." Here the connection between the God's means of provision for the Hebrews in the wilderness and his means of provision for us could not be clearer. We must be sustained by partaking of Jesus.

How do we do this? I think there are several ways and the different traditions of Christianity emphasize different means of God's grace. For the more sacramental streams, the teaching here is clear: we partake of Christ through the elements of the Lord's Supper. Even for those traditions that take a less sacramental view of Communion, the truth that we should partake of Christ is clearly represented in the practice. Just as God's means of creation is the basis for the practice of baptism, the truth about the way God sustains us on our journey is the basis for the practice of Communion. At its institution,

> [Jesus] took bread, and when he had given thanks, he broke it and said, "This is my body, which is for you; do this in remembrance of me." In the same way, after supper he took the cup, saying, "This cup is the new covenant in my blood; do this, whenever you drink it, in remembrance of me." For whenever you eat this bread and drink this cup, you proclaim the Lord's death until he comes. (1 Cor. 11:24-25)

As for other ways of partaking of Jesus, I would suggest that, among other spiritual disciplines that people may practice, certainly prayer and Bible Study are non-negotiable. In Deut. 8:3 God explains that he led the people into the wilderness so that they would become hungry and that he could teach them that they do not live by bread alone, but by the Word of God. The Word of God comes to us in many ways: including the Word of God administered (the sacraments) and the Word of God incarnate (Jesus). But there is also the Word of God inspired (scripture) and we must not neglect this vital means of knowing God and appropriating his strength.

I have often heard people say something to the effect of "I feel guilty because I haven't been reading my Bible or praying much lately." Guilty? Why would you feel guilty? That is like saying I feel guilty for missing dinner last night. If I miss a meal, I don't feel guilty, I feel hungry. Prayer and Bible study is spiritual food. If I am not partaking in it, I should feel hungry, not guilty. I know that there have been several periods in my life when I have felt spiritually weak. Almost invariably, one reason has been my like of prayer and Bible study. Perhaps it is the language we use that causes us to think about this incorrectly. After all, the idea of practicing spiritual disciplines does seem closely akin to practicing physical disciplines. Reading the Bible is likened to working out at the gym. This is actually a decent and biblical notion. We should train ourselves to be godly using divinely ordered means (See, for example, 1 Tim. 4:7-8). However, we must be careful not to take this notion too far, because missing out on prayer and Bible study is not really like eating too many sweets one day or skipping out on exercise. It is much more like not drinking water or not eating, because it is a matter of growth and survival, not just getting into top shape. Being in good shape is an option that some of us choose to forfeit, for whatever reason. (A lot of us are perfectly satisfied being a bit out of shape, right?) We can decide to skip that trip to the fitness center and still get along in life. That is not the case with eating. We cannot skip all our meals and expect everything to be alright. We need sustenance.

That is what Communion and prayer and Bible study are. They are food for our eternal souls. God grants us new life at the Red Sea and continued life through the desert, so as we journey across that hot and dusty land, let's not try to attempt it without the food and water that is Jesus Christ.

Chapter 5

The Reason for the Rules

The Purpose of the Law

If I were to ask random people on the street to name one event that happened to the Israelites between Egypt and the Promised Land, I suspect that most (among those that could answer at all, of course) would name the giving of the Ten Commandments on Mt. Sinai, and for good reason. This was a pivotal moment in history. In the handing down of the law (not just the commandments but the rest of the 613 rules as well), God revealed his moral will for the people of Israel. If we want to know how God wants us to live, this is as good a place as any to start. Unfortunately, from the very beginning, people have been starting with the rules and ending up at the wrong place. They have been getting the wrong answer about what God wants from them.

The problem is that we misunderstand why God gave us the rules. We tend to think that he gave us the law to show us what righteousness looks like. In other words, we see the rules as an end in and of themselves. In this view, to be righteous is to keep the rules. How do I know I am a good person in the eyes of God? Because I keep the rules.

For example, within this understanding of the law, I could put Exodus 20 up on my wall and read it every night to evaluate how I've done that day. Did I murder anyone today? Nope. Check. Did I steal anything? No. Check. Did I have sex with anyone who wasn't my wife? Negative. Check. Did I make or worship any statues? Not that I remember. Check. And on down the line. As long as I can check off everything (or at least most things) on the list of rules, I must be pretty righteous, right?

This is a mistake. The law is not an end in and of itself. It cannot be used as a checklist for measuring holiness. Rather, the law is a means to a different end: inner righteousness; godly character. The rules are not intended to be an indicator or true holiness; they are designed to lead us to true holiness. To be truly righteous is to be a particular type of person. It is to exhibit certain inner character qualities. It is not just about keeping the rules.

Adding Rules upon Rules

Unfortunately, using commandments as a checklist for righteousness is very common. One reason for this is that it offers a straightforward and easy way of not only gauging one's righteousness, but of making oneself appear and feel more and more righteous. This is done by adding and keeping more commandments that are even in the Bible!

For instance, every church sub-culture seems to have many extra-biblical rules (written or unwritten) that people follow. "Come to church a certain number of times per week;" "Serve in some capacity such as teaching Sunday School;" "Wear a certain type of clothing;" "Listen to a particular style of music;" "Don't drink or smoke," etc. I once visited a church that had every congregant's name on a list in the foyer. Beside each name was a row of boxes to check, each representing an activity that the people were to have taken part in the previous week. Did you read your Bible twice a day? Check. Did you evangelize at least five people this week? Check. Did you give your offering? Check. These things were seen as a sign of being righteousness, even though they are not explicitly commanded by God anywhere. However, they do provide an easy way to quantify whether or not you a good person? "Why, I am an elder of the church board and told twenty people about God last week, for goodness sake. How much more holy can I get?"

Redefining the Rules
Treating the rules as a yardstick for holiness is also popular because it makes it easy to interpret the law in such a way as to allow for stuff that we want to do. So if the law says I am not to gossip or lie about my neighbor, I can say, "Well, I didn't lie and gossip about my neighbor – the person I was talking about was two doors down." A lot of teenagers I know have very explicit physical relationships with their boyfriends and girlfriends yet believe that they are doing nothing wrong because they didn't actually have intercourse. They define fornication in such a way that they can have sex without actually having sex. Convenient isn't it?

Being, not Doing
These two approaches to the rules may be popular, but they are simply wrong. While the rules are good in and of themselves - keeping them is better than not keeping them for many practical reasons (the law against murder keeps people safe, for example, and it is certainly it is good to go to church and teach Sunday School and evangelize) - their primary function is to lead. One is not righteous simply by keeping those rules or any of the other regulations we come up with. Rather, we become righteous as we mature and develop the character qualities that God possesses. Holiness is not about *doing* certain things; it is about *being* – being like Christ.

Unfortunately, the legalistic approach to the rules has been around ever since God handed them down. Jesus addressed this mindset in much of his teaching, including his most famous discourse, the Sermon on the Mount. Just as God gave the people the rules from a mountain, Jesus climbed up on one to explain those rules more clearly (Matthew 5:1, 17-20). He started with the sixth commandment:

> You have heard that it was said to the people long ago, "Do not murder, and anyone who murders will be subject to judgment." But I tell you that anyone who is angry with his brother will be subject to judgment. Again, anyone who says to his brother, "Raca," is answerable to the Sanhedrin. But anyone who says, "You fool!" will be in danger of the fire of hell. (Matthew 5:21-22)

Not only are we not to kill one another, Jesus says, but we are not even supposed to get angry with each other. We can't go to the rule list at the end of the day and check off number 6 and think we are doing all right. Instead of asking, "Did I kill anyone today?" we have to ask, "What was my attitude toward other people today?" This gets to the heart of the issue. God doesn't just want to keep you from murdering someone; he wants you to be a forgiving, loving person. God desires a heart condition that is not quantifiable. The rule about murder is to be followed, yes, but it is not the end of the issue. Rather, it is a means to a further end. That end is a pure heart.

Jesus continued: "You have heard that it was said, 'Do not commit adultery.' But I tell you that anyone who looks at a woman lustfully has already committed adultery with her in his heart" (Matthew 5:27-28). Jesus says that it is not enough just to not have sex with someone who is not your spouse. You are not even to lust. You are to be a faithful person in your heart. You are to use the law to develop a character quality, not treat it as a task to be check marked.

Jesus goes on to address the character qualities of honesty and trustworthiness.

> Again, you have heard that it was said to the people long ago, "Do not break your oath, but keep the oaths you have made to the Lord." But I tell you, Do not swear at all: either by heaven, for it is God's throne; or by the earth, for it is his footstool; or by Jerusalem, for it is the city of the Great King. And do not swear by your head, for you cannot make even one hair white or black. Simply let your "Yes" be "Yes," and your "No," "No"; anything beyond this comes from the evil one. (Matthew 5:33-37)

The religious leaders of Jesus' time had developed a system of rules to elaborate on the injunction to "keep your oaths." The list explained when a person had to keep their word and when it was OK not to. If one swore "by the earth" it meant one thing, and if the same person swore "by Jerusalem" it meant another, for example. It was a bit like the rules that grade school students use to test credibility: to "pinky swear" means a vow must be kept, but if fingers were crossed at the time of the promise, it doesn't need to be kept.

Jesus cuts through that nonsense by saying that we are simply to be trustworthy people. Keeping our word is not a matter of doing what the law says; it is about being a certain type of person. Jesus implies that if we have to use an oath to back up our promise, there is a problem already. If we tell someone we are going to do something and then have to follow that up with "I swear," it is probably an indication that we have let that person down in the past and are not entirely trustworthy.

In the next passage, Jesus' teaching gets radical.

You have heard that it was said, "Eye for eye, and tooth for tooth." But I tell you, Do not resist an evil person. If someone strikes you on the right cheek, turn to him the other also. And if someone wants to sue you and take your tunic, let him have your cloak as well. If someone forces you to go one mile, go with him two miles. Give to the one who asks you, and do not turn away from the one who wants to borrow from you.

You have heard that it was said, "Love your neighbor and hate your enemy." But I tell you: Love your enemies and pray for those who persecute you, that you may be sons of your Father in heaven. He causes his sun to rise on the evil and the good, and sends rain on the righteous and the unrighteous. If you love those who love you, what reward will you get? Are not even the tax collectors doing that? And if you greet only your brothers, what are you doing more than others? Do not even pagans do that? Be perfect, therefore, as your heavenly Father is perfect. (Matthew 5:38-48)

The background for this part of the sermon is the idea that justice should be proportionate. The rules stated that if someone harmed another person, they were due that amount of harm in return and not more, while those that treated people well were due that friendship in return. The goal was to keep acts of vengeance from escalating out of control. The idea was to keep people from killing each other over name-calling, for example. An eye for an eye was enough, an eye and a leg for an eye was too much. Justice was encouraged, disproportionate vengeance was not. However, Jesus says even avoiding vengeance is not enough. The rule was meant to push people to an even higher standard. We are to be the kind of people who actually love our enemies and seek their good. In short, we should be perfect. This is God's will.

A Parental Approach to the Rules

My wife and I have a list of rules for our children. For example, they are not allowed to hit each other, they have to wash their hands before meals, and they must say "please" and "thank you" at the appropriate times. We have several reasons for these rules, including our desire to keep them safe from harm and diseases. However, one reason we do not have is the desire for them to grow up and be proud of how polite or clean they are. These rules are not to be used as indicators of righteousness.

We don't want our daughter to grow up and think to herself (or say to anyone else), "I am such a cultured person. Look at how polite and well groomed I am. Why, I don't even hit other people." In fact, that is just the opposite of what we want. These rules are in place to keep the kids humble, not to make them proud. We want them to say "please" as a sign of gratitude and "thank you" as a sign of respect. The rule is designed to point their attention away from themselves and towards the person they are addressing. In the same way, we have a rule about praying before meals. It is intended to generate and keep an attitude of thankfulness to God as we acknowledge our dependence on him. If the prayers turn into displays of self-aggrandizement ("Look at how many flowery words I can say in my prayer," etc), the rule is being misused.

While we strictly enforce the rule about not hitting, it is not a license for the kids to pinch ("But I didn't *hit* her!"). It is also not an indication that we want the children to cease touching each other at all ("You said I can't hit so I am never going to hug her again either!") We want the interpersonal relationship rules to guide the children toward actually caring about the well-being of their siblings. In the same way, personal hygiene rules are intended to engender a respect for one's body and a desire for healthy living. The heart condition is what is ultimately important; the rules are primarily a means to that end.

This is what Jesus explained in his sermon. The Old Testament law was given to the world for the same reason that rules are given to children: to lead them toward righteousness of the heart. The rules are to be kept, but are not the end-all and be-all of righteousness. Character is. The rules are for children. When a child grows up he or she should no longer need the rules to tell them what to do. Rather, they should be the kind of people that the rules meant for them to be. For example, if my child who is now four continues to say her prayers and say "please" and "thank you" only out of obedience to me when she is 25, there is a problem. By that time she should be mature enough, humble enough and thankful enough to do those things because they flow naturally from who she is. I don't expect my son, who is now a toddler, to have to call me up when he is thirty to ask me how he should treat a co-worker who won't share. He should be well beyond that. That is the point: rules are necessary for the immature, but as a person grows, they shouldn't need the rules anymore. The rules should have served their purpose and become superfluous. That is how God uses the rules as well. They are meant to lead us to being people of character.

Paul sums up this principle well and provides us a nice list of qualities in Galatians 5: "The fruit of the Spirit is love, joy, peace, forbearance, kindness, goodness, faithfulness, [23] gentleness and self-control.

Against such things there is no law" (Galatians 5:22-23). Notice that fruit of the Spirit consists entirely of character qualities. Also, look how Paul ends the list: against such things there is no law! Why is there no law? Because the law is for those who have not developed character qualities yet. The rules are for children, for the immature. When one grows up, the law is no longer needed.

Jesus' Warning to the Pharisees
The Pharisees and teachers of the law are prominent in the gospels for their misunderstanding of the law. Again and again Jesus scolded them, with this passage providing a good summary of his points:

> Woe to you, teachers of the law and Pharisees, you hypocrites! You give a tenth of your spices— mint, dill and cumin. But you have neglected the more important matters of the law—justice, mercy and faithfulness. You should have practiced the latter, without neglecting the former. You blind guides! You strain out a gnat but swallow a camel.

> Woe to you, teachers of the law and Pharisees, you hypocrites! You clean the outside of the cup and dish, but inside they are full of greed and self-indulgence. Blind Pharisee! First clean the inside of the cup and dish, and then the outside also will be clean.

> Woe to you, teachers of the law and Pharisees, you hypocrites! You are like whitewashed tombs, which look beautiful on the outside but on the inside are full of dead men's bones and everything unclean. In the same way, on the outside you appear to people as righteous but on the inside you

are full of hypocrisy and wickedness. (Mathew 23:23-28)

It doesn't get any clearer than that. Righteousness is not keeping the letter of the law in an outward show of obedience; it is a heart condition. Righteousness is qualitative, not quantitative. The Pharisees were very good at checking items off their daily list of rules and duties, but they missed the point. Notice that Jesus tells them they have "neglected the more important matter of the law – justice, mercy and faithfulness." This is just what we have been saying. God wants us to be a certain type of person: one that is just and merciful and faithful. As God explains in Hosea 6:6, "I desire mercy not sacrifice, acknowledgment of God rather than burnt offerings" God does not need a percentage of our possessions as if that offering was good in and of itself. He desires that we be righteous on the inside.

Applying This Principle to Acts of Service
This principle applies not only to the keeping of the law and to spiritual disciplines, but to all of our acts of service. The Sermon on the Mount concludes with a very scary passage about the final judgment:

> Not everyone who says to me, "Lord, Lord," will enter the kingdom of heaven, but only he who does the will of my Father who is in heaven. Many will say to me on that day, "Lord, Lord, did we not prophesy in your name, and in your name drive out demons and perform many miracles?" Then I will tell them plainly, "I never knew you. Away from me, you evildoers!" (Matt. 7:21-23)

The people that come to Jesus have a nice checklist of rules they have obeyed. They believed the right things

("Lord, Lord" is the proper confession) and they have been actively and effectively serving God. Clearly they expect to be welcomed into Heaven with open arms. However, Jesus says that they have not been doing his will. How can this be? What is Jesus' will in this passage? From the context of the sermon, we know that Jesus wants them to "bear fruit" (Matt. 7:15-20) and that bearing fruit is to produce the proper character qualities, to be the right kind of person. Why does Jesus not approve of these people? Because, even while serving him, they are evildoers. They do not have the inner righteousness that God desires.

This is a problem that Paul addresses in explaining that even the greatest acts of ministry in the world are pointless if they are not done by a loving person:

> If I speak in the tongues of men and of angels, but have not love, I am only a resounding gong or a clanging cymbal. If I have the gift of prophecy and can fathom all mysteries and all knowledge, and if I have a faith that can move mountains, but have not love, I am nothing. If I give all I possess to the poor and surrender my body to the flames, but have not love, I gain nothing.
>
> Love is patient, love is kind. It does not envy, it does not boast, it is not proud. It is not rude, it is not self-seeking, it is not easily angered, it keeps no record of wrongs. Love does not delight in evil but rejoices with the truth. It always protects, always trusts, always hopes, always perseveres. (1 Corinthians 13:1-7)

It is easy to get into the habit of quantifying our spiritual life. We judge our righteousness by how many activities we can cram into our busy schedule. Look back at the list of actions we made at the beginning of this chapter. If you practice them, do you see them as duties to be checked off a list each week or do they flow from your heart? May we always remember that the Christian enterprise is about making people holy, not keeping them busy.

I once visited a church with a traveling ministry team. We pulled up in front of the building and jumped out of our van to unload equipment and ask for specific directions. Before we could do any of that, though, the senior pastor came out and screamed at us for parking in the wrong spot. I couldn't believe what a jerk the guy was. That pastor had the biggest church in town, with programs that ran like well-oiled machines. He had all the outward trappings of successful religion but (at least on that day) he neglected the more important matter of inner righteousness displayed in mercy and patience. He did not love us.

Judgment Day

We don't want to show up on judgment day saying, "Look at all we did" like the people in the "Lord, Lord" passage of Matthew 7. Instead we should hope to stand before God like the people Jesus talks about in Matthew 25.

> When the Son of Man comes in his glory, and all the angels with him, he will sit on his throne in heavenly glory. All the nations will be gathered before him, and he will separate the people one from another as a shepherd separates the sheep from the goats. He will put the sheep on his right and the goats on his left.

Then the King will say to those on his right, "Come, you who are blessed by my Father; take your inheritance, the kingdom prepared for you since the creation of the world. For I was hungry and you gave me something to eat, I was thirsty and you gave me something to drink, I was a stranger and you invited me in, I needed clothes and you clothed me, I was sick and you looked after me, I was in prison and you came to visit me."

Then the righteous will answer him, "Lord, when did we see you hungry and feed you, or thirsty and give you something to drink? When did we see you a stranger and invite you in, or needing clothes and clothe you? When did we see you sick or in prison and go to visit you?"

The King will reply, "I tell you the truth, whatever you did for one of the least of these brothers of mine, you did for me." (Matt 25:31-40)

Notice that the people who make it into Heaven in this passage had also been busy working. However, the difference between these folks and the "evildoers" of Matthew 7 is the servants in Matthew 25 didn't focus on the deeds as an end in themselves. Indeed, they didn't focus on them at all – they couldn't even remember doing them. This shows that they were just the type of people who helped others in need. They were loving, kind, generous and humble. They weren't looking at their works with pride or as an indicator of their righteousness. These are the kind of people Jesus welcomes into the Promised Land. These people have the character traits he is looking for. On the other hand, if they had shown up and said, "Look at how we worked in the homeless shelter, Lord," they would have been rejected for having the wrong approach to service.

Conclusion

We are not to obey the rules as an end in themselves but because they are a means toward helping us become righteous people. God handed down the commandments to help develop character, not as the benchmark of character. The mark of a disciple is not busyness, but holiness. True righteousness is the goal of redemption. Developing character is an absolutely essential part of our journey. As Peter argues, we must continue to possess character qualities in ever increasing measure, always becoming more and more like Jesus.

> His divine power has given us everything we need for life and godliness through our knowledge of him who called us by his own glory and goodness. Through these he has given us his very great and precious promises, so that through them you may participate in the divine nature and escape the corruption in the world caused by evil desires.
>
> For this very reason, make every effort to add to your faith goodness; and to goodness, knowledge; and to knowledge, self-control; and to self-control, perseverance; and to perseverance, godliness; and to godliness, brotherly kindness; and to brotherly kindness, love. For if you possess these qualities in increasing measure, they will keep you from being ineffective and unproductive in your knowledge of our Lord Jesus Christ. But if anyone does not have them, he is nearsighted and blind, and has forgotten that he has been cleansed from his past sins. (2 Peter 1:3-9)

Chapter 6

The Seriousness of Sin

Sin is No Big Deal, Right?

I spent the last chapter trying to convince you that the main point of the law is character development and I concluded by saying that holiness is an "essential part of our journey." I'm going to take the next two chapters to emphasize the word *essential*. I often get the impression that people think developing holiness is like living the "Extra Special Deluxe" edition of the Christian life. It's nice and all, but you don't *really* need it. These people have the idea that actually becoming like Jesus is OK for really fanatical people, but for the vast majority, a more moderate approach is just fine. This attitude is revealed in sentiments like, "It is so great that God is a God of grace and that it doesn't really matter what kind of lives we live. So I gossip a little here or cut a few ethical corners there, God still loves me." You see it in statements such as, "I know that what I am doing is wrong, but we are about grace here, not judgment," and even in the bumper sticker slogan I mentioned earlier: "I'm not perfect, just forgiven." As I explained in Chapter 1, this is the attitude that I had for much of my younger years.

These sayings are promoting the idea, one that has become pervasive in many churches, that sin is simply not that big of a deal. The underlying assumption is that it does not matter if you sin because sin has no *ultimate* significance. Sin does not keep you from having a relationship with God, and it certainly doesn't keep you from getting to Heaven, so why worry about it? If righteousness fanatics and mediocre sinners all end up in the same place anyway, there is simply not much motivation to diligently pursue righteousness. In fact, diligently pursuing holiness is sometimes scorned within this framework. The "regular folk" look down on those who are not content to live in ethical mediocrity as "overly zealous," like the people who not only get the deluxe package, but then outfit their new SUV with 24 karat gold wheels. Can't you hear the whispering? "Now that's just ostentatious. Can't those people stop showing off and just be plain like the rest of us? I am so glad that I can be content with who I am."

I think the idea that sin has no really severe consequences is a major reason that so many polls reveal the morality of Christians to be essentially the same as the morality of non-Christians.[17] or example, studies have found that some 40% of pastors consume porn on a regular basis.[18] Speaking of evangelicals in particular, but making a statement that is applicable across the Christian spectrum, Michael Horton laments: "Christians are as likely to embrace lifestyles every bit as hedonistic, materialistic, self-centered, and sexually immoral as the world in general."[19]

Is this a big deal? Is sin serious? Where does holiness come into the plan of salvation? Is it necessary? Does everyone end up in the same place regardless of their moral quality?

Let's start answering these questions by looking at how Peter finished the train of thought he started in the passage with which we concluded Chapter 5. He explained that we should be adding righteous character qualities to our lives and then ended by pointing out the important ramifications of continuing to become holy: "Therefore, my brothers, be all the more eager to make your calling and election sure. For if you do these things, you will never fall, and you will receive a rich welcome into the eternal kingdom of our Lord and Savior Jesus Christ" (2 Peter 1:10-11).

According to Peter, as long as you are growing in righteousness, you will never fall and will receive a rich welcome into Heaven. But what is the implication if you are not becoming like Jesus? A plain-sense reading of the text suggests that those who do not grow in righteousness are in danger of falling and not receiving a rich welcome in the eternal Kingdom. I believe that is correct. In explaining the benefits of growing in righteousness, Peter is also issuing a warning about the peril of not growing in righteousness. In this chapter I will expand on this warning and argue that the reason growing in righteousness is so important is that sin, *at any stage in your journey to the Promised Land*, causes a rift in your relationship with God and puts you in danger of not making it into Heaven. Only those who persevere in their relationship with God and thereby grow in holiness all the way to the end of the expedition get in. Holiness is not an "add-on" to the Christian life. It is not the leather seats or gold wheels, which are nice but unessential. Rather, righteousness is the essential standard equipment. It is the chassis and the engine. You can't get across the wilderness without it.

Warnings from the Exodus Story

As it has throughout our study, the Exodus story provides us with our primary illustration of this truth. Many Israelites started out on the journey to the Promised Land, but very few actually finished and made it in. Even though these Hebrews escaped Egypt, passed through the Red Sea and experienced God's miraculous provision in the desert, sin brought them down. As Paul clearly explains, this is an illustration of what can happen to Christians who allow sin to keep them from finishing the journey. After calling on his readers to run the race to the end and fight the war in such a way as to win rather than to lose, he explains why:

For I do not want you to be ignorant of the fact, brothers, that our forefathers were all under the cloud and that they all passed through the sea. They were all baptized into Moses in the cloud and in the sea. They all ate the same spiritual food and drank the same spiritual drink; for they drank from the spiritual rock that accompanied them, and that rock was Christ. Nevertheless, God was not pleased with most of them; their bodies were scattered over the desert.

Now these things occurred as examples to keep us from setting our hearts on evil things as they did. Do not be idolaters, as some of them were; as it is written: "The people sat down to eat and drink and got up to indulge in pagan revelry." We should not commit sexual immorality, as some of them did – and in one day twenty-three thousand of them died. We should not test the Lord, as some of them did – and were killed by snakes. And do not grumble, as some of them did – and were killed by the destroying angel.

These things happened to them as examples and were written down as warnings for us, on whom the fulfillment of the ages has come. So, if you think you are standing firm, be careful that you don't fall! (1 Corinthians 10:1-12)

The importance of the Exodus story in understanding the gospel of Jesus doesn't get any clearer than that! Paul says that the Israelite's journey through the Red Sea was symbolic of the baptism that a Christian undergoes at the beginning of his or her journey. This is just what we have been saying. To get to the Promised

Land, the Israelites had to be freed from the power of Pharaoh and the penalty of God's judgment and walk out of Egypt under the blood of the lamb. To get to Heaven we need to be freed from Satan's power and the penalty of God's judgment by getting under the blood of our lamb, Jesus. We then are baptized and begin the next stage of the journey home, just as the Israelites were baptized in the Red Sea as they began a new stage in their journey. After making these connections, Paul explicitly states that we are to learn from the Israelites' example so that we don't repeat their mistake and "fall." Paul doesn't want us to end up dead in the wilderness rather than home in the Promised Land.

So what exactly did the Israelites do? Paul references several events, beginning with perhaps the most severe. "The people sat down to eat and drink and got up to indulge in pagan revelry" is a quote from Exodus 32, a chapter explaining what happened as the people were waiting for Moses to come down from Mount Sinai. They built the golden calf. The episode concludes with Moses trying to make atonement for the people.

> The next day Moses said to the people, "You have committed a great sin. But now I will go up to the LORD; perhaps I can make atonement for your sin."

> So Moses went back to the LORD and said, "Oh, what a great sin these people have committed! They have made themselves gods of gold. But now, please forgive their sin—but if not, then blot me out of the book you have written."

> The LORD replied to Moses, "Whoever has sinned against me I will blot out of my book. Now go, lead the people to the place I spoke of, and my

angel will go before you. However, when the time comes for me to punish, I will punish them for their sin."

And the LORD struck the people with a plague because of what they did with the calf Aaron had made. (Exodus 32:1-35)

The people succumbed to idolatry and God blotted them out of his book. They made it out of Egypt, but they died in the desert due to sin. Why was God so harsh? The bottom line is that sin leads to death. Always.

Sin Equals Death

Satan's biggest lie is that if we sin we "will not surely die" (Genesis 3:4). He used it on Adam and Eve in the Garden of Eden and has continued to try it on every person since. As our first parents and the Israelites learned the hard way, Satan is wrong. The truth is, "The wages of sin is death" (Romans 6:23).

Relationships are based on a covenant of trust. Breaking that covenant breaks relationship. Sinning against God breaks relationship with him in the same way that lying to or cheating on one's spouse breaks relationship with him or her. One cannot commit adultery and think that everything is going to remain all right. Trust has been broken and a schism is the result. This is exactly what happens when we sin against God. Adam and Eve were kicked out of the Garden of Eden and the Children of Israel were not allowed to enter the Promised Land. Breaking relationship with God keeps us from his presence and being out of the presence of God is hell. Literally.

Now you might say, "But, Don, look at the rest of Romans 6:23. The wages of sin may be death, but 'the gift of God is eternal life in Christ Jesus our Lord.' Doesn't that mean that our sin is now covered, or at least can be covered, by Jesus?"

This idea is common and often arises in the context of using this text as an evangelistic tool. People quote it to potential converts in explaining that although everyone sins and is deserving of death, God gives Christians the gift of eternal life through Jesus instead. This is a severe misuse of this text. These teachers are essentially paraphrasing the verse something like this: "The wages of sin for an unbeliever is death, but a Christian can sin without consequence because of Jesus." The only way to reach this understanding is to insert a conditional timeline to the principle that sin equals death: "The wages of sin used to be death for me, but since I came to Jesus I have become exempt from that rule."

These interpretations are completely unwarranted and in fact result in a teaching that is *exactly the opposite* of what Paul intended. Paul is not telling non-Christians that they can escape the penalty of current sins by turning to Jesus. He is writing to Christians with a warning that they are not to use God's grace as a license to sin because the unchangeable rule of the universe is that sin leads to death! This becomes apparent when you look at the rest of Romans 6.

You No Longer Have to Sin, So Don't

Paul's argument in the first part of Romans 6 can be summarized, "Since Christ has enabled us to live righteous lives we should no longer sin." Again and again Paul rails against sin, explaining that since Christ has set us free, we should no longer live as slaves.

> What shall we say, then? Shall we go on sinning so that grace may increase? By no means! We

died to sin; how can we live in it any longer? Or don't you know that all of us who were baptized into Christ Jesus were baptized into his death? We were therefore buried with him through baptism into death in order that, just as Christ was raised from the dead through the glory of the Father, we too may live a new life.

If we have been united with him like this in his death, we will certainly also be united with him in his resurrection. For we know that our old self was crucified with him so that the body of sin might be done away with, that we should no longer be slaves to sin – because anyone who has died has been freed from sin.

Now if we died with Christ, we believe that we will also live with him. For we know that since Christ was raised from the dead, he cannot die again; death no longer has mastery over him. The death he died, he died to sin once for all; but the life he lives, he lives to God.

In the same way, count yourselves dead to sin but alive to God in Christ Jesus. Therefore do not let sin reign in your mortal body so that you obey its evil desires. Do not offer the parts of your body to sin, as instruments of wickedness, but rather offer yourselves to God, as those who have been brought from death to life; and offer the parts of your body to him as instruments of righteousness. For sin shall not be your master, because you are not under law, but under grace. (Romans 6:1-14)

Paul then adds some serious emphasis to his point by reminding his readers of the consequences of sin. He points out that the penalty for sin is still the same as it always has been: death. Since nobody should want death, especially when life is offered to them through Jesus, they should stop sinning and accept life. As you read the rest of the passage, notice the formula Paul uses in contrasting our two options:

Sin = Separation from God (Death)
Grace (Being Set Free) = Obedience, Righteousness, Holiness = Eternal Life

Sin is always associated directly with death, and God's grace is always associated directly with righteousness, which is linked directly to eternal life.

What then? Shall we sin because we are not under law but under grace? By no means! Don't you know that when you offer yourselves to someone to obey him as slaves, you are slaves to the one whom you obey – whether you are slaves to sin, which leads to death, or to obedience, which leads to righteousness? But thanks be to God that, though you used to be slaves to sin, you wholeheartedly obeyed the form of teaching to which you were entrusted. You have been set free from sin and have become slaves to righteousness.

I put this in human terms because you are weak in your natural selves. Just as you used to offer the parts of your body in slavery to impurity and to ever-increasing wickedness, so now offer them in slavery to righteousness leading to holiness. When you were slaves to sin, you were free from the control of righteousness. What benefit did you reap at that time from the things you are now ashamed of? Those things result in death! But now that you have been set free from sin and have become slaves to God, the benefit you reap leads to holiness, and the result is eternal life. For the wages of sin is death, but the gift of God is eternal life in Christ Jesus our Lord. (Romans 6:15-23)

So Paul's full argument in Romans 6 is that Jesus has set us free from having to sin, which is good because sin leads to death. Because of Jesus' work, we are now able to live righteously, which is also good, because holiness leads to eternal life. Therefore, we should choose life by living holy lives! Don't sin, lest we die!

The fact is, sin leads to death; it separates us from God. This is a hard and fast rule of the universe. It applies to everyone. As Isaiah explained (to believers), "Your iniquities have separated you from your God; your sins have hidden his face from you" (Isaiah 59:2). That is why the writer of Hebrews can say, "Without holiness, *no one* will see the Lord" (Hebrews 12:14, emphasis mine).

It is easy to emphasize the importance of God's forgiveness in salvation, but we must not forget that forgiveness is just the first step in the process. Becoming holy is part of the plan, too. Jesus didn't come just to forgive sin; he came to eradicate it. His goal for us is holiness.

For example, when faced with a woman caught in adultery, Jesus didn't condemn her. However, he didn't tell her that everything was alright, either. Sin was her problem and, he told her to get rid of it.

Jesus bent down and started to write on the ground with his finger. When [the religious leaders who had brought the woman before Jesus] kept on questioning him, he straightened up and said to them, "If any one of you is without sin, let him be the first to throw a stone at her." Again he stooped down and wrote on the ground.

At this, those who heard began to go away one at a time, the older ones first, until only Jesus was left, with the woman still standing there. Jesus straightened up and asked her, "Woman, where are they? Has no one condemned you?"

"No one, sir," she said.

"Then neither do I condemn you," Jesus declared. "Go now and leave your life of sin." (John 8:7-11)

Jesus had a similar message for the man he healed at the pool of Bethesda. Jesus said to him, "See, you are well again. Stop sinning or something worse may happen to you" (John 5:14).

Jesus saw the danger of sin so clearly that he even recommended, hyperbolically, self-mutilation as a reasonable alternative. After all, it is better to lose a hand than be sent to hell.

> If your right eye causes you to sin, gouge it out and throw it away. It is better for you to lose one part of your body than for your whole body to be thrown into hell. And if your right hand causes you to sin, cut it off and throw it away. It is better for you to lose one part of your body than for your whole body to go into hell. (Matthew 5:29-30)

Here, Jesus clearly equated sinning with entering Hell. If Hell is defined as separation from God, and sin separates, then Jesus was making the point of this chapter exactly.

Jesus' forgiveness is always accompanied by a call to holiness. It is one thing to make it through Passover, to be covered by the blood of the lamb and escape punishment. It is quite another thing to make it across the wilderness. The wilderness is the spiritual formation part of the journey, where we are made into the type of person God wants us to be. The two segments of the journey can never be separated. Eternal life cannot be obtained by stopping at Passover or the Red Sea or Mount Sinai. We must not stop at being forgiven by Jesus. We must also become holy.

Depending on your theological background, you now might be thinking, "But what about the most famous verse in the Bible? What about John 3:16: 'For God so loved the world that he gave his one and only Son, that whoever believes in him shall not perish but have eternal life.'? There doesn't seem to be anything about holiness in there."

There is, actually, if you look at the context. This verse is in a passage in which Jesus explains to Nicodemus what is required for eternal life. Jesus tells Nicodemus that he must be born again (John 3:3). By this Jesus meant that Nicodemus had to become a completely new person, one who was born of the spirit rather than flesh (John 3:5-7). This is what we talked about in Chapter 1.

God's intent is that we be holy. There is no contingency in his mission for this not to take place. There is no backup route to the Promised Land for those who do not become righteous. The Nicodemus passage concludes with stark moral language contrasting those who get eternal life with those who don't. Those who hang on to their evil deeds are left in the darkness.

This is the verdict: Light has come into the world, but men loved darkness instead of light because

their deeds were evil. Everyone who does evil
hates the light, and will not come into the light for
fear that his deeds will be exposed. But whoever
lives by the truth comes into the light, so that it
may be seen plainly that what he has done has
been done through God. (John 3:19-21)

Is righteousness important? Yes! Is sin a big deal?
Yes! These verses from John 3 state the exact formula
we talked about from Romans 6. They simply add some
more descriptive terminology to it.

Sin (Living According to Flesh) = Separation from
God (Death)
Grace (Being Born Again, Living According to the
Spirit) = Holiness = Eternal Life

The fact that living by the Spirit is characterized by
holiness is a strong New Testament theme. For instance,
Paul contrasts life in the flesh and life in the spirit by
focusing on the different moral characteristics of each.

So I say, live by the Spirit, and you will not gratify
the desires of the sinful nature. For the sinful
nature desires what is contrary to the Spirit, and
the Spirit what is contrary to the sinful nature.
They are in conflict with each other, so that you
do not do what you want. But if you are led by the
Spirit, you are not under law.

The acts of the sinful nature are obvious: sexual
immorality, impurity and debauchery; idolatry and
witchcraft; hatred, discord, jealousy, fits of rage,
selfish ambition, dissensions, factions and envy;
drunkenness, orgies, and the like. I warn you, as I

did before, that those who live like this will not inherit the kingdom of God.

But the fruit of the Spirit is love, joy, peace, patience, kindness, goodness, faithfulness, gentleness and self-control. Against such things there is no law. Those who belong to Christ Jesus have crucified the sinful nature with its passions and desires. (Galatians 5:16-24)

The mark of a true follower of Christ, one who is living by the Spirit, is holiness. On the other hand, a life lived apart from the Spirit is easily discernible by its unrighteousness. Notice the strong language of Ephesians 5. Paul makes a point of declaring that immoral people do not get into the Kingdom, and for this reason we should strive to live righteously by the Spirit.

Be imitators of God, therefore, as dearly loved children and live a life of love, just as Christ loved us and gave himself up for us as a fragrant offering and sacrifice to God.

But among you there must not be even a hint of sexual immorality, or of any kind of impurity, or of greed, because these are improper for God's holy people. Nor should there be obscenity, foolish talk or coarse joking, which are out of place, but rather thanksgiving. For of this you can be sure: No immoral, impure or greedy person – such a man is an idolater – has any inheritance in the kingdom of Christ and of God Let no one deceive you with empty words, for because of such things God's wrath comes on those who are disobedient. Therefore do not be partners with them.

For you were once darkness, but now you are light in the Lord. Live as children of light (for the fruit of the light consists in all goodness, righteousness and truth) and find out what pleases the Lord. Have nothing to do with the fruitless deeds of darkness, but rather expose them. For it is shameful even to mention what the disobedient do in secret. But everything exposed by the light becomes visible, for it is light that makes everything visible. This is why it is said: "Wake up, O sleeper, rise from the dead, and Christ will shine on you."

Be very careful, then, how you live – not as unwise but as wise, making the most of every opportunity, because the days are evil. Therefore do not be foolish, but understand what the Lord's will is. Do not get drunk on wine, which leads to debauchery. Instead, be filled with the Spirit. (Ephesians 5:1-18)

In the second to last chapter in the Bible, Jesus explains who will inherit eternal life and who will not. Notice the categories he uses. Those who overcome get the Kingdom while the wicked are sent to Hell. Jesus again makes plain that righteousness is imperative, and sin cannot be tolerated.

[Jesus] said to me: "It is done. I am the Alpha and the Omega, the Beginning and the End. To him who is thirsty I will give to drink without cost from the spring of the water of life. He who overcomes will inherit all this, and I will be his

God and he will be my son. But the cowardly, the unbelieving, the vile, the murderers, the sexually immoral, those who practice magic arts, the idolaters and all liars – their place will be in the fiery lake of burning sulfur. This is the second death." (Revelation 21:6-8)

"But Nobody's Perfect"

Before moving on, I want to address one more possible objection to the argument presented in this chapter. You might be thinking something like this: "But Don, this picture is too bleak. Nobody's perfect. We all sin. According to your logic, we are all going to end up in Hell."

Well, hopefully not. It is certainly true that everyone sins. It is also true that some of these sinners will go to Heaven. The key to reconciling this apparent contradiction is to remember that broken relationships can be restored through confession and forgiveness. While sin separates us from God, repentant confession of that sin combined with God's forgiveness enables that relationship to continue growing.

The Apostle John describes how this works in his first epistle. In the passage below, he starts by affirming the point we have been making about the necessity of righteousness.

> This is the message we have heard from him and declare to you: God is light; in him there is no darkness at all. If we claim to have fellowship with him yet walk in the darkness, we lie and do not live by the truth. But if we walk in the light, as he is in the light, we have fellowship with one another, and the blood of Jesus, his Son, purifies us from all sin. (1 John 1:5-7)

John says that true believers walk in the light and are purified from sin. Those who continue their life of unrighteousness do not live in the light or by the truth. Basically, John argues that Christians should be living holy lives. However, he realizes that nobody is perfect and anticipates the objection we have raised, so he explains what to do when we fall short: confess our sins.

> If we claim to be without sin, we deceive ourselves and the truth is not in us. If we confess our sins, he is faithful and just and will forgive us our sins and purify us from all unrighteousness. If we claim we have not sinned, we make him out to be a liar and his word has no place in our lives.
>
> My dear children, I write this to you so that you will not sin. But if anybody does sin, we have one who speaks to the Father in our defense – Jesus Christ, the Righteous One. He is the atoning sacrifice for our sins, and not only for ours but also for the sins of the whole world. (1 John 1:8-2:2).

John tells us to deal with sin by admitting to God that we are sinners and throwing ourselves on his mercy, making use of the reconciliation that is now possible through Jesus. This act of confession is more than just telling God the facts of our situation, of course. The type of confession John is talking about flows from a penitent heart. There is no room here for the kind of "confession" that says "I can do whatever I want on Saturday night because Sunday morning I will confess and be forgiven." That is to use God's grace as a license for sin and is strongly condemned (see our discussion on Romans 6 above). The proper confessional attitude is exemplified by a tax collector in one of Jesus' parables:

To some who were confident of their own righteousness and looked down on everybody else, Jesus told this parable: "Two men went up to the temple to pray, one a Pharisee and the other a tax collector. The Pharisee stood up and prayed about himself: 'God, I thank you that I am not like other men – robbers, evildoers, adulterers – or even like this tax collector. I fast twice a week and give a tenth of all I get.'

"But the tax collector stood at a distance. He would not even look up to heaven, but beat his breast and said, 'God, have mercy on me, a sinner.'

"I tell you that this man, rather than the other, went home justified before God. For everyone who exalts himself will be humbled, and he who humbles himself will be exalted." (Luke 18:9-14)

Everyone who confesses their sins in the manner of the tax collector will have those sins forgiven. John wants us to know that. However, as soon as he has made that point, he makes sure that we understand that this concession to the reality of sin is not a license to continue in sin. Right after explaining confession, John goes back to his main point: don't sin. Although have an avenue for forgiveness in the event of sin, the bottom line is that a lifestyle of sin is a mark of an unbeliever and must not be tolerated by a follower of Christ. The very next passage in the epistle makes this clear:

We know that we have come to know him if we obey his commands. The man who says, "I know him," but does not do what he commands is a liar, and the truth is not in him. But if anyone obeys his word, God's love is truly made complete in him. This is how we know we are in him: Whoever claims to live in him must walk as Jesus did. (1 John 2:3-6)

Nobody is perfect. However, we should all be striving for perfection. Becoming holy is a process, and the mark of a true believer is progressively greater righteousness. We may not be completely righteous, but we should be becoming more and more righteous. This is the point Peter makes in the passage with which we concluded the last chapter:

> Make every effort to add to your faith goodness; and to goodness, knowledge; and to knowledge, self-control; and to self-control, perseverance; and to perseverance, godliness; and to godliness, brotherly kindness; and to brotherly kindness, love. For if you possess these qualities in increasing measure, they will keep you from being ineffective and unproductive in your knowledge of our Lord Jesus Christ. (2 Peter 1:5-8)

We should have Paul's attitude:

> But whatever was to my profit I now consider loss for the sake of Christ. What is more, I consider everything a loss compared to the surpassing greatness of knowing Christ Jesus my Lord, for whose sake I have lost all things. I consider them rubbish, that I may gain Christ and be found in him, not having a righteousness of my own that comes from the law, but that which is through faith in Christ – the righteousness that comes from

God and is by faith. I want to know Christ and the power of his resurrection and the fellowship of sharing in his sufferings, becoming like him in his death, and so, somehow, to attain to the resurrection from the dead.

Not that I have already obtained all this, or have already been made perfect, but I press on to take hold of that for which Christ Jesus took hold of me. Brothers, I do not consider myself yet to have taken hold of it. But one thing I do: Forgetting what is behind and straining toward what is ahead, I press on toward the goal to win the prize for which God has called me heavenward in Christ Jesus. (Philippians 3:7-14)

Paul was striving to be perfect. He had not become perfect yet, but nothing less would satisfy. Paul wanted to be like Christ.

Sinful acts are symptomatic of an improper heart condition and constant exhibition of these acts without confession and repentance shows that a person is not being changed. On the other hand, a righteous person is continually growing in holiness and is truly repentant when sin occurs. In fact, a penitent heart shows that one is truly hungering and thirsting for righteousness.

Jesus came to free us not only from the penalty of sin, but from the power of sin as well. He wants to make you and me into a certain type of person. That is what the journey is all about.

Righteousness is not optional in the plan of redemption. Unfortunately, many people seem to think it is. A.W. Pink bemoaned the situation early in the twentieth century, and his critique is still valid.

The nature of Christ's salvation is woefully misrepresented by the present-day evangelist. He announces a Savior from Hell rather than a Savior from sin. And that is why so many are fatally deceived, for there are multitudes who wish to escape the Lake of fire who have no desire to be delivered from their carnality and worldliness.[20]

We will close this chapter with a quotation from the great preacher, Charles Spurgeon, who also emphasized the necessity of righteousness:

Christ will be master of the heart, and sin must be mortified. If your life is unholy, then your heart is unchanged, and you are an unsaved person. The Savior will sanctify His people, renew them, give them a hatred of sin, and a love of holiness. The grace that does not make a man better than others is a worthless counterfeit. Christ saves His people, not IN their sins, but FROM their sins. Without holiness, no man shall see the Lord.[21]

Chapter 7

The Necessity of Perseverance

The Golden Calf, Revisited

Because it is such an important episode in the Exodus story, I want to use this chapter to speak more about the Israelites' worship of the golden calf. Last chapter I described their problem as "falling into sin" and warned that sin must be avoided because it leads to death. I want to make essentially the same point in this chapter, but in two slightly different ways, corresponding to two slightly different ways of describing what happened at the base of Mount Sinai. Along with explaining the Israelites' rebellion as "falling into sin," we can also say that they "failed to make it to the end of the journey" and they "failed to be prepared for Moses' return from the top of the mountain." These distinctions are subtle, but I think this chapter will show you the value in making them. The biblical authors certainly saw it. They consistently referenced the story of the disobedient Israelites in warning us to persevere all the way to the end of our journey and to be prepared for the return of Christ. We will first look at biblical exhortations to persevere, followed by warnings to be ready.

Biblical Exhortations to Persevere

As we discussed last chapter, sin separates from God. Whether we have never walked with God or have journeyed far toward the Promised Land, this law of the universe still applies. For this reason, we must constantly be on guard against sin, because the devil wants nothing more than to knock us off the narrow path. According to Peter, he "prowls around like a

roaring lion looking for someone to devour" (1 Peter
5:8). As such, the Bible is filled with warnings to
persevere in the battle and finish the race. We are to
"resist him, standing firm in the faith" (1 Peter 5:9).
We have already seen the call to perseverance in 2
Peter 1:3-11 (at the end of Chapter 5), and 1 Corinthians
10:1-12 (at the beginning of Chapter 6); there are many
more passages that make the same point. For example,
the writer of Hebrews looks back at how the Israelites
allowed sin to sidetrack them as part of his argument
encouraging his readers to "hold on to the courage of
which we boast" (Hebrews 3:6):

> So, as the Holy Spirit says: "Today, if you hear his
> voice, do not harden your hearts as you did in the
> rebellion, during the time of testing in the desert,
> where your fathers tested and tried me and for
> forty years saw what I did. That is why I was
> angry with that generation, and I said, 'Their
> hearts are always going astray, and they have not
> known my ways.' So I declared on oath in my
> anger, 'They shall never enter my rest.'"

> See to it, brothers, that none of you has a sinful,
> unbelieving heart that turns away from the living
> God. But encourage one another daily, as long as
> it is called Today, so that none of you may be
> hardened by sin's deceitfulness. We have come to
> share in Christ if we hold firmly till the end the
> confidence we had at first. As has just been said:
> "Today, if you hear his voice, do not harden your
> hearts as you did in the rebellion."

> Who were they who heard and rebelled? Were
> they not all those Moses led out of Egypt? And
> with whom was he angry for forty years? Was it

not with those who sinned, whose bodies fell in the desert? And to whom did God swear that they would never enter his rest if not to those who disobeyed? So we see that they were not able to enter, because of their unbelief. (Hebrews 3:7-19)

The author then admonishes us to take heed and do better than the Israelites who did not enter the Promised Land. "Therefore, since the promise of entering his rest still stands, let us be careful that none of you be found to have fallen short of it" (Hebrews 4:1). He concludes by encouraging us to "hold firmly to the faith we profess" (Hebrews 4:14).

In the next two chapters, the warnings about falling away from the faith become even more explicit:

> It is impossible for those who have once been enlightened, who have tasted the heavenly gift, who have shared in the Holy Spirit, who have tasted the goodness of the word of God and the powers of the coming age, if they fall away, to be brought back to repentance, because to their loss they are crucifying the Son of God all over again and subjecting him to public disgrace.

> Land that drinks in the rain often falling on it and that produces a crop useful to those for whom it is farmed receives the blessing of God. But land that produces thorns and thistles is worthless and is in danger of being cursed. In the end it will be burned.

> Even though we speak like this, dear friends, we are confident of better things in your case—things that accompany salvation. (Hebrews 6:4-8)

Although the writer is hopeful, the warnings are deadly serious. A life on the path of salvation always produces good fruits, which, as we have explained previously, are godly character qualities. A sojourner that fails to exhibit these qualities is in danger of being cursed. As is explained later in Hebrews, it will be dreadful for those God has to judge in this way:

> Let us draw near to God with a sincere heart in full assurance of faith, having our hearts sprinkled to cleanse us from a guilty conscience and having our bodies washed with pure water. Let us hold unswervingly to the hope we profess, for he who promised is faithful. And let us consider how we may spur one another on toward love and good deeds. Let us not give up meeting together, as some are in the habit of doing, but let us encourage one another—and all the more as you see the Day approaching.

If we deliberately keep on sinning after we have received the knowledge of the truth, no sacrifice for sins is left, but only a fearful expectation of judgment and of raging fire that will consume the enemies of God. Anyone who rejected the law of Moses died without mercy on the testimony of two or three witnesses. How much more severely do you think a man deserves to be punished who has trampled the Son of God under foot, who has treated as an unholy thing the blood of the covenant that sanctified him, and who has insulted the Spirit of grace? For we know him who said, "It is mine to avenge; I will repay," and again, "The Lord will judge his people." It is a dreadful thing to fall into the hands of the living God.

Remember those earlier days after you had received the light, when you stood your ground in a great contest in the face of suffering. Sometimes you were publicly exposed to insult and persecution; at other times you stood side by side with those who were so treated. You sympathized with those in prison and joyfully accepted the confiscation of your property, because you knew that you yourselves had better and lasting possessions.

So do not throw away your confidence; it will be richly rewarded. You need to persevere so that when you have done the will of God, you will receive what he has promised. For in just a very little while, "He who is coming will come and will not delay. But my righteous one will live by faith. And if he shrinks back, I will not be pleased with him." But we are not of those who shrink back and are destroyed, but of those who believe and are saved. (Hebrew 10:22-39)

Hopefully so. Races must be finished and battles must be won. There is no consolation prize for those who don't make it to the end of a journey and to finish second in war is to lose. There is no Promised Land for those who don't persevere in righteousness. After giving many examples of great heroes of faith who persevered even in the face of great persecution, the writer of Hebrews sums up the call: "Therefore, since we are surrounded by such a great cloud of witnesses, let us throw off everything that hinders and the sin that so easily entangles, and let us run with perseverance the race marked out for us" (Hebrews 12:1).
John exhorts,

> See that what you have heard from the beginning remains in you. If it does, you also will remain in the Son and in the Father. And this is what he promised us – even eternal life.
>
> I am writing these things to you about those who are trying to lead you astray. As for you, the anointing you received from him remains in you, and you do not need anyone to teach you. But as his anointing teaches you about all things and as that anointing is real, not counterfeit—just as it has taught you, remain in him. (1 John 2:24-29)

To remain in Jesus is to follow him and not turn back. As Jesus explained to a would-be disciple, Heaven is not for quitters. A man came to Jesus and said, "'I will follow you, Lord; but first let me go back and say good bye to my family.' Jesus replied, 'No one who puts his hand to the plow and looks back is fit for service in the kingdom of God'" (Luke 9:61-62).

Later in Luke we find Jesus warning his listeners that becoming a disciple is not a short-term commitment. Following Jesus requires following him to the end. Jesus told the people crowding around him to examine themselves and decide if they were willing to do that. Jesus asks, "If you start this, will you be able to finish it?"

> Large crowds were traveling with Jesus, and turning to them he said: "If anyone comes to me and does not hate his father and mother, his wife and children, his brothers and sisters—yes, even his own life—he cannot be my disciple. And anyone who does not carry his cross and follow me cannot be my disciple.

"Suppose one of you wants to build a tower. Will he not first sit down and estimate the cost to see if he has enough money to complete it? For if he lays the foundation and is not able to finish it, everyone who sees it will ridicule him, saying, 'This fellow began to build and was not able to finish.'

"Or suppose a king is about to go to war against another king. Will he not first sit down and consider whether he is able with ten thousand men to oppose the one coming against him with twenty thousand? If he is not able, he will send a delegation while the other is still a long way off and will ask for terms of peace. In the same way, any of you who does not give up everything he has cannot be my disciple.

"Salt is good, but if it loses its saltiness, how can it be made salty again? It is fit neither for the soil nor for the manure pile; it is thrown out.

"He who has ears to hear, let him hear." (Luke 14:25-35)

Notice the salt reference at the end. Disciples of Jesus can start out salty but lose their flavor and become useless. No wonder Jesus said to "Listen up." This is very serious stuff.

Paul was so concerned about it that he openly worried that he might have wasted his efforts with the believers in Galatia.

Formerly, when you did not know God, you were slaves to those who by nature are not gods. But now that you know God – or rather are known by

> God – how is it that you are turning back to those weak and miserable principles? Do you wish to be enslaved by them all over again? You are observing special days and months and seasons and years! I fear for you, that somehow I have wasted my efforts on you. (Galatians 4:8-11)

Apparently the Galatians had been "running a good race," but now someone had "cut in on them" (Galatians 5:7) and "thrown them into confusion" (Galatians 5:10). After then describing the characteristics of a righteous person (the fruits of the Spirit, which we covered in Chapter 8), Paul emphasizes why they need to persevere in righteousness:

> Do not be deceived: God cannot be mocked. A man reaps what he sows. The one who sows to please his sinful nature, from that nature will reap destruction; the one who sows to please the Spirit, from the Spirit will reap eternal life. Let us not become weary in doing good, for at the proper time we will reap a harvest if we do not give up. Therefore, as we have opportunity, let us do good to all people, especially to those who belong to the family of believers. (Galatians 6:7-10)

We must persevere in becoming righteous and not give up. As Paul told Titus, "The Lord delivered his people out of Egypt, but later destroyed those who did not believe" (Titus 6). We must not be like those Israelites. We are to "fight the good fight" and "hold on to faith and a good conscience" (1 Timothy 1:18-19), not "shipwreck our faith" as others have done (1 Timothy 1:20). "If we endure, we will also reign with him. If we disown him, he will also disown us; if we are faithless, he will remain faithful, for he cannot disown himself" (2 Timothy 2:12-13).

The Return of Moses and the Return of Christ

In our discussion of the Israelites' lapse into idolatry at the foot of Mount Sinai, we have looked at explicit biblical warnings against sin (Chapter 9) and admonitions to persevere in righteousness to the end of the journey (the first part of this chapter). The Hebrews failed on both counts when they worshipped the golden calf. They fell into sin and did not make it into the Promised Land. Now I want to talk about a third way to understand their failure: They were not ready for Moses' return.

As we already read, much of the impetus for building the calf came from impatience with Moses. The Israelites didn't have anybody watching over them, so they went their own way: "When the people saw that Moses was so long in coming down from the mountain, they gathered around Aaron and said, 'Come, make us gods who will go before us. As for this fellow Moses who brought us up out of Egypt, we don't know what has happened to him'" (Exodus 32:1). Aaron relented, and the Israelites were subsequently unprepared to meet Moses when he finally did come down the mountain.

This is another episode in which Moses is a type of Christ. Just as the Children of Israel should have remained faithful and been ready for Moses' return, we are to be ready for Jesus when he comes back. The Bible assures us that, just as Moses came down from the mountain and meted out justice, Jesus will return to earth and do the same. In the spirit of some of the great judgment days of the past, the return of Christ will be unexpected and severe:

Just as it was in the days of Noah, so also will it be in the days of the Son of Man. People were eating, drinking, marrying and being given in marriage up to the day Noah entered the ark. Then the flood came and destroyed them all.

It was the same in the days of Lot. People were eating and drinking, buying and selling, planting and building. But the day Lot left Sodom, fire and sulfur rained down from heaven and destroyed them all.

It will be just like this on the day the Son of Man is revealed. On that day no one who is on the roof of his house, with his goods inside, should go down to get them. Likewise, no one in the field should go back for anything. Remember Lot's wife! Whoever tries to keep his life will lose it, and whoever loses his life will preserve it. I tell you, on that night two people will be in one bed; one will be taken and the other left. Two women will be grinding grain together; one will be taken and the other left. (Luke 17:26-35)

The biblical authors use the fact of Christ's return as one more motivation for persevering in righteousness. For example, just after the passages we already read in 1 John that warn of the inherent dangers of sin and appeal to us to "remain in Jesus" (1 John 2:27), John makes the same plea with a slightly different impetus. This time he emphasizes that Jesus is coming back, and we don't want to be caught unprepared and ashamed on that day: "And now, dear children, continue in him, so that when he appears we may be confident and unashamed before him at his coming" (1 John 2:28).

Two Kinds of Readiness for Two Types of Events

Before we examine more biblical passages that warn us to be ready, I think it will be helpful to look briefly at the nature of readiness. Readiness is about being prepared for a future event. However, different categories of events require different types of readiness. We need to understand what type of event the coming of Jesus is so that we can prepare for it accordingly. I think there are many people who think they are ready to meet Jesus but simply are not because they have been preparing for the wrong kind of event.

There are at least two categories of future events. The first I will call the "Natural Disaster" category. This type of event would include earthquakes, hurricanes, and floods. To prepare for these events, people might do such tasks as secure bookshelves, reinforce walls and over-passes, board up windows, build up levees, purchase insurance, and perhaps evacuate if given enough warning.

There are two things to notice about the events in this category. The first is that preparing for them involves doing jobs that can be completed. The work required for preparation can be finished. You can reach a point where you just sit back and say, "I am prepared, at least as prepared as I want to be." For example, the hurricane is coming, but everyone in the city has evacuated and is sitting in hotel rooms 500 miles away, watching the coverage on TV, doing nothing but waiting.

The second thing to notice is that unless you go and undo what has already been done, you never become unready. People who are prepared for the storm remain ready while doing nothing more. Sitting in the hotel room just watching TV is not going to cause you to become less prepared. The windows stay boarded. After the checklist is completed, your readiness level remains the same. If the pantry has been filled with nonperishable food and medical supplies, it stays filled. It does not need to be continually re-stocked as you wait for an earthquake.

Of course, natural disasters are not the only type of events that fit into this category. Think about being ready for a vacation. The car is serviced and full of gas, the bags are packed, the travel insurance purchased, the route mapped out, the dog sitter scheduled, and the passport renewed. Every task on the pre-trip checklist is finished, and you are able to relax on the couch the night before the trip and say "I am prepared." The same principles apply. You were able to finish all the tasks, and are not going to become unready as you sit on the couch or sleep. Preparation is done. Now you just wait.

The second type of events fall into what I am going to call the "Unscheduled Return of the Boss to Work" category. A typical future event of this type would be the return of a supervisor from vacation or lunch at an undisclosed time. What does it take to be ready? Keeping busy. In order to be prepared for this event, you need to be sure to have enough work to do and then you need to keep doing it. The key to being ready when the boss pops in is to not be slacking off.

Here is what to notice about being ready for this category of events. First, it involves tasks that must be continually performed until the event occurs. You need to work at being ready right up until the time it happens. The job is never completed. You can never rest and must always be vigilant.

Although there are tasks involved that can be completed, such as upgrading the computer so it won't crash or making coffee to drink to keep energized, finishing those tasks only enables you to continue working. There's no saying to the boss "I *was* working but my printer ran out of ink, so I quit." Nor would it be wise to say, "I filled up the ink cartridges on the printer

and figured that was good enough, so I called it a day."
In both cases the manager will consider you unready for
his or her return.

In this category of events there is no point where you
can say, "I'm finished. I've done all I can. I am now
completely ready for the person in charge to return."
Instead, it is necessary to watch, to work, and to be
prepared to watch and work for the long haul.

The second thing to notice about readiness for these
types of events is that you can be ready at one point and
then stop being ready. As long as you are performing the
necessary tasks, you are ready, but as soon as you stop
working, you become unready. Have you ever stayed
busy right up until two minutes before your supervisor
came back and then decided that one quick game of
computer solitaire wouldn't hurt? You may have been
ready up until two minutes before his or her return, but
if the boss caught you playing cards, you weren't ready.

Another example of a future event that fits into this
category is a terrorist attack. How do airports, for
example, or buildings such as the White House prepare
for a potential attack from terrorists? While they do
some tasks that can be completed, such as installing
concrete road blocks to keep cars at a distance,
ultimately they would be less than secure if they did not
also post guards to keep watch. These sentries are
responsible to keep an around-the-clock lookout for
suspicious activity. If the watchmen fall asleep on the
job or don't show up for work, places like airports and
the White House stop being ready. The same principle
of readiness applies.

A final example of an "Unscheduled Return of the
Boss" type of event is a bridal entrance. To be ready for
a bride to make her appearance at a wedding, you have
to be watching for her. You may have already
accomplished many tasks to be ready for that moment

(showering, traveling to the wedding site, purchasing a gift, etc.), but if you are not watching for the bride to enter, you are not ready.

This actually happened to me recently. My wife and I attended an outdoor wedding in a beautiful Southern California location. We found our seats among a large group of old friends that we had not seen for a while, and everyone started visiting. Because of the acoustics of the setting, the music accompanying the ceremony was very hard to hear, and in the midst of our talking and laughing, we did not notice the wedding start. By the time we realized what was happening, most of the wedding party had already marched down the aisle and was waiting at the front for the bride. As everyone stood up to welcome her, we finally took notice. We were not ready, much to our embarrassment.

So again, readiness for this type of event involves tasks that must be continually performed until the event occurs. One must work at being prepared right up until the time the event happens. The work is never completed. There is no rest; one must always be vigilant.

That difference between the two categories of events is clearly seen in the answer to the question: "How do we know we are ready for a future event?" In the "Natural Disaster" category we would say, "We have accomplished certain tasks" or at least, "Certain tasks have already been accomplished." In the "Boss Returning to Work" category we would say, "We have performed certain tasks or certain tasks have been accomplished, *and* we are performing certain tasks and are prepared to perform them (or at least have them performed) indefinitely."

The Big Question

With this understanding of the nature of readiness as a background, we come to the big question: Which type of event is the return of Christ?

People often speak of Jesus' return as if it was a natural disaster. They talk of being ready using references to things accomplished in the past: "Jesus died for me. I asked him into my heart. Both of these events are done. My insurance is purchased, my windows are boarded up, and my bookshelves are securely fastened to the wall. I'm ready. I can rest. Hurricane Jesus is on the way, but all that can be done is done. I will be spared."

Jesus, however, never talked about being ready for his return in this sense. He never spoke of himself as anything like a hurricane or referred to being prepared for his return as if it was some kind of natural disaster. He did, however, in the context of teaching about his return, often refer to himself as a master, a thief and a bridegroom, metaphors that coincide precisely with being a boss, a terrorist and a bride. According to Jesus, his return fits perfectly into our second category of future events.

For example, in warning his disciples about the coming judgment at his return, Jesus compared himself to a master of household servants:

> No one knows about that day or hour, not even the angels in heaven, nor the Son, but only the Father. Be on guard! Be alert! You do not know when that time will come. It's like a man going away: He leaves his house and puts his servants in charge, each with his assigned task, and tells the one at the door to keep watch.

> Therefore keep watch because you do not know when the owner of the house will come back – whether in the evening, or at midnight, or when the rooster crows, or at dawn. If he comes suddenly, do not let him find you sleeping. What I say to you, I say to everyone: 'Watch!' (Mark 13:32-37)

It is clear which type of event this is. Jesus is the boss making an unscheduled return.

In a similar warning, Jesus compared himself to a thief in the night. The arrival of a burglar is to be treated exactly as we would treat a terrorist attack: with constant watchfulness:

> Therefore keep watch, because you do not know on what day your Lord will come. But understand this: If the owner of the house had known at what time of night the thief was coming, he would have kept watch and would not have let his house be broken into. So you also must be ready, because the Son of Man will come at an hour when you do not expect him. (Matthew 24:42-44)

Jesus then proceeded immediately to another story in which he is the master returning to his servants.

> Who then is the faithful and wise servant, whom the master has put in charge of the servants in his household to give them their food at the proper time? It will be good for that servant whose master finds him doing so when he returns. I tell you the truth, he will put him in charge of all his possessions. But suppose that servant is wicked and says to himself, "My master is staying away a long time," and he then begins to beat his fellow

servants and to eat and drink with drunkards. The master of that servant will come on a day when he does not expect him and at an hour he is not aware of. He will cut him to pieces and assign him a place with the hypocrites, where there will be weeping and gnashing of teeth. (Matthew 24:45-51)

Then, just in case his listeners had not yet apprehended the point, Jesus compared himself to a bridegroom, another person whose coming must be prepared for with constant vigilance.

At that time the kingdom of heaven will be like ten virgins who took their lamps and went out to meet the bridegroom. Five of them were foolish and five were wise. The foolish ones took their lamps but did not take any oil with them. The wise, however, took oil in jars along with their lamps. The bridegroom was a long time in coming, and they all became drowsy and fell asleep.

At midnight the cry rang out: "Here's the bridegroom! Come out to meet him!"

Then all the virgins woke up and trimmed their lamps. The foolish ones said to the wise, "Give us some of your oil; our lamps are going out."

"No," they replied, "there may not be enough for both us and you. Instead, go to those who sell oil and buy some for yourselves."

But while they were on their way to buy the oil, the bridegroom arrived. The virgins who were ready went in with him to the wedding banquet. And the door was shut.

Later the others also came. "Sir! Sir!" they said. "Open the door for us!"

But he replied, "I tell you the truth, I don't know you."

Therefore keep watch, because you do not know the day or the hour. (Matthew 25:1-13)

In one teaching episode, Jesus used all the metaphors. He pulled together images of a boss and a thief and even threw in a reference to a wedding banquet, perhaps to remind his listeners of his other lessons on this subject.

"Be dressed ready for service and keep your lamps burning, like men waiting for their master to return from a wedding banquet, so that when he comes and knocks they can immediately open the door for him. It will be good for those servants whose master finds them watching when he comes. I tell you the truth, he will dress himself to serve, will have them recline at the table and will come and wait on them. It will be good for those servants whose master finds them ready, even if he comes in the second or third watch of the night. But understand this: If the owner of the house had known at what hour the thief was coming, he would not have let his house be broken into. You also must be ready, because the Son of Man will come at an hour when you do not expect him."

Peter asked, "Lord, are you telling this parable to us, or to everyone?"

The Lord answered, "Who then is the faithful and wise manager, whom the master puts in charge of his servants to give them their food allowance at the proper time? It will be good for that servant whom the master finds doing so when he returns. I tell you the truth, he will put him in charge of all his possessions. But suppose the servant says to himself, 'My master is taking a long time in coming,' and he then begins to beat the menservants and maidservants and to eat and drink and get drunk. The master of that servant will come on a day when he does not expect him and at an hour he is not aware of. He will cut him to pieces and assign him a place with the unbelievers." (Luke 12:35-46)

In all of his teachings, Jesus spoke of his return as an event that belongs in our second category. There is not a single example of Jesus telling us to prepare for his return as though it is natural disaster type of event. We are not to prepare as if the coming of Jesus is like a hurricane or earthquake, but rather as if the returning Jesus is like a thief or a boss coming back to the jobsite. Jesus tells his followers to be continually working, always watching, constantly on guard. Disciples are to never stop doing this; they are not to fall asleep. To be ready for Jesus means to keep busy until he returns, not rely on past actions. There is no point at which anyone can say, "I have done everything I need to do to be ready, and my preparation is complete." Rather, we must persevere in our work to the end.

The rest of the New Testament echoes the Gospels in teaching this principle. For example, Paul told the Thessalonians, "Now, brothers, about times and dates we do not need to write to you, for you know very well that the day of the Lord will come like a thief in the night. While people are saying, 'Peace and safety,' destruction will come on them suddenly, as labor pains on a pregnant woman, and they will not escape" (1 Thessalonians 5:1-3).

Being ready for Jesus is not a matter of having a nice list of past experiences to refer back to. It is a matter of working and watching for Him right now. It is a matter of growing in righteousness until the very moment we die or he returns. It means not falling asleep on the job. Living holy lives to the end is essential. Peter paints a very clear picture:

> But the day of the Lord will come like a thief. The heavens will disappear with a roar; the elements will be destroyed by fire, and the earth and everything in it will be laid bare.

> Since everything will be destroyed in this way, what kind of people ought you to be? You ought to live holy and godly lives as you look forward to the day of God and speed its coming. That day will bring about the destruction of the heavens by fire, and the elements will melt in the heat. But in keeping with his promise we are looking forward to a new heaven and a new earth, the home of righteousness.

> So then, dear friends, since you are looking forward to this, make every effort to be found spotless, blameless and at peace with him. Bear in mind that our Lord's patience means salvation, just as our dear brother Paul also wrote you with the wisdom that God gave him. He writes the same way in all his letters, speaking in them of these matters. His letters contain some things that

are hard to understand, which ignorant and unstable people distort, as they do the other Scriptures, to their own destruction.

Therefore, dear friends, since you already know this, be on your guard so that you may not be carried away by the error of lawless men and fall from your secure position. But grow in the grace and knowledge of our Lord and Savior Jesus Christ. To him be glory both now and forever! Amen. (2 Peter 3:10-18)

The potential for falling from a secure position is exactly what worried Jesus about the church in Sardis. He declared through John that they needed to wake up and follow the example of those who overcome and do not get their names blotted out of the Book of Life.

To the angel of the church in Sardis write: These are the words of him who holds the seven spirits of God and the seven stars. I know your deeds; you have a reputation of being alive, but you are dead. Wake up! Strengthen what remains and is about to die, for I have not found your deeds complete in the sight of my God. Remember, therefore, what you have received and heard; obey it, and repent. But if you do not wake up, I will come like a thief, and you will not know at what time I will come to you. Yet you have a few people in Sardis who have not soiled their clothes. They will walk with me, dressed in white, for they are worthy. He who overcomes will, like them, be dressed in white. I will never blot out his name from the book of life, but will acknowledge his name before my Father and his angels. He who has an ear, let him hear what the Spirit says to the churches. (Revelation 3:1-6)

Conclusion

The Israelites who worshipped the golden calf got their names blotted out of the book because they:

a. Fell into sin
b. Did not persevere to the end of the journey
c. Were not prepared for Moses' return

These are, of course, just three ways of saying the same thing: sin is a very big deal at every stage in our journey and must be avoided at all costs. There will always be sin that needs to be confessed, as we discussed in Chapter 6, but we should constantly be growing in holiness. We should always be changing more and more into the type of person described in Chapter 5. We are not to let the length of the journey or its inherent hardships cause us to sin. As Jesus warned, don't let the things of this life keep you from being continually ready to meet him.

> Be careful, or your hearts will be weighed down with dissipation, drunkenness and the anxieties of life, and that day will close on you unexpectedly like a trap. For it will come upon all those who live on the face of the whole earth. Be always on the watch, and pray that you may be able to escape all that is about to happen, and that you may be able to stand before the Son of Man. (Luke 21:34-36)

Philosopher Dallas Willard rightly complains that today's church seems to spend a lot of time trying to get people's papers in order for heaven instead of fostering relationship with Jesus and true discipleship that results in holiness.[22] I hope that is not true of us. We don't want to be people (or be a church that produces people) who prepare for Jesus' return as if it was a hurricane. We don't want to be found on that great and mighty day of the Lord with a list of safety measures we completed years ago or an insurance contract in our hand saying, "Remember me? Remember when you signed this? I finished what you wanted me to do a long time ago. I'm sure glad I got that taken care of then and didn't have to do anything else because frankly, life got a little busy."

Instead, we want to be people who are able to greet Jesus as a benevolent master. When he appears, we should, setting aside what we have been doing for the kingdom, be able to run up to Jesus with a big hug and say, "I've been expecting you." We should be people who can rightly expect to hear him say, "I know my child. Well done, good and faithful servant."

Chapter 8

God with Us

Not Going Alone

So far on our study, the Children of Israel have not been doing very well. They failed badly when they complained about food and water and then botched it again in building a golden calf. By that point, it looks like God had had enough. He told Moses to continue leading the people to the Promised Land, but God was not going to go with them "because you are a stiff-necked people and I might destroy you on the way" (Exodus 33:3). God would send an angel instead. Moses doubted that he would be able to succeed on this mission and cried out to God in discouragement. (Exodus 33:12-13)

I am sure we can understand Moses' frustration. The journey is long and hard, and humans seem ill-equipped to carry it out. The call to persevere in holiness that we discussed in the previous two chapters may have left you unsure about your prospects. "I don't think I can do it" seems to me a perfectly normal response. God understands this, just like he understood Moses' concern. In his grace, he gave Moses a helper: God himself.

> The LORD replied, "My Presence will go with you, and I will give you rest."
>
> Then Moses said to him, "If your Presence does not go with us, do not send us up from here. How will anyone know that you are pleased with me and with your people unless you go with us? What

else will distinguish me and your people from all
the other people on the face of the earth?"

And the LORD said to Moses, "I will do the very
thing you have asked, because I am pleased with
you and I know you by name." (Exodus 33:14-17)

God made success on the journey possible by actually
coming down and traveling with the Israelites. In this
chapter we will examine what that looked like and then
see how God does the same thing for us.

God's Tabernacle

As sojourners in the wilderness, the Israelites
obviously did not have any permanent dwellings in
which to live. However, they did not leave themselves
completely open to the elements. They carried along
portable tent-like structures. These booths, or
tabernacles, were basically poles covered by flexible
material like cloth or animal hides. These shelters
provided protection and easy portability.

When God decided to come and travel with the
Israelites across the wilderness, he ordered them to build
for him a portable structure to inhabit: his tabernacle
(Exodus 25:8). You can find the explicit architectural
instructions for this building in Exodus Chapters 25
through 30 and the account of the building process in
Exodus Chapters 35 through 40. When they were
finished, a cloud covered the tent "and the glory of the
Lord filled the tabernacle" (Exodus 40:34).

The book of Exodus then concludes,

In all the travels of the Israelites, whenever the
cloud lifted from above the tabernacle, they would
set out; but if the cloud did not lift, they did not set
out – until the day it lifted. So the cloud of the

LORD was over the tabernacle by day, and fire was in the cloud by night, in the sight of all the house of Israel during all their travels. (Exodus 40:36-38)

Although there is much we could say about the tabernacle, for our purposes I will focus on the fact that in order to get the people across the wilderness, God came down and dwelt in the same type of portable home as they were living in. He condescended to help the Israelites by leaving his heavenly home to reside with them in their temporary shelters.

God's presence provided the people with guidance and protection. With the cloud and the fire always in view over the tabernacle, they could be assured that they were safe and on the right track. If ever doubts arose about the chances of making it across the wilderness successfully, the people could gain assurance from the knowledge that God was with them.

The Feast of Tabernacles

In later years, after the Israelites were settled in the Promised Land, they were commanded to commemorate this aspect of the journey by holding the Festival of Tabernacles, also known as the Feast of Booths or *Sukkot* in Hebrew. (Deuteronomy 16:13-15). Here are God's directions for the festival as recorded in Leviticus.

So beginning with the fifteenth day of the seventh month, after you have gathered the crops of the land, celebrate the festival to the LORD for seven days; the first day is a day of rest, and the eighth day also is a day of rest. On the first day you are to take choice fruit from the trees, and palm fronds, leafy branches and poplars, and rejoice before the LORD your God for seven days. Celebrate this as a festival to the LORD for seven days each year. This is to be a lasting ordinance for the generations to come; celebrate it in the seventh month. Live in booths for seven days: All native-born Israelites are to live in booths so your descendants will know that I had the Israelites live in booths when I brought them out of Egypt. I am the LORD your God. (Leviticus 23:39-43)

To this day certain Jews celebrate the Festival of Tabernacles by building portable huts outside their permanent homes and living in them for a full week. As they celebrate the harvest and God's continued provision and protection, they remember a time when God provided for them in temporary shelters and protected them when they were sojourners in the wilderness. They recall how God provided manna for them from Heaven and water from the rock, and they especially remember how God journeyed with them across the wilderness by inhabiting his own temporary shelter, his own tabernacle.

Jesus' Birthday

To begin my explanation of what all this information means to us, I am going to argue that Jesus was born on the first day of the Feast of Tabernacles. While I am not interested in canceling Christmas or giving up celebrating Jesus' birth in December each year, I think there are many good reasons to think it actually occurred on *Sukkot,* and that this date provides a depth of meaning to the event that December 25th simply does not.

Let's start by establishing the date of John the Baptist's birth with some simple number crunching. John's father Zechariah was a priest serving on duty in the temple when the angel Gabriel appeared to him to tell him that he would have a son (Luke 1:8). We know from Luke 1:5 that Zechariah belonged to the priestly division of Abijah. From this bit of information we can nail down almost exactly what time of year the angel appeared him and then deduce from that when Jesus was born. To do so, however, we will need some background in the Jewish priestly system.

Priests served in the temple in teams, with each team serving for one week at a time (1 Chronicles 9), two times a year. The teams were scheduled to serve in a certain order each year, and 1 Chronicles 24:7-18 explains that the division of Abijah was the 8th team of the year. This was called the eighth course.

Along with their two weeks of individual priestly service, all the priests would report to the temple and serve together three times a year during the Feast of Weeks, the Feast of Unleavened Bread and the Feast of Booths (Deuteronomy 16:16). The total number of weeks served in the temple by each priest, then, was five.

Because the Feast of Unleavened Bread and the Feast of Weeks both occur within the first eight weeks of the Jewish year, the eighth course would have served during the tenth week of the year (approximately Sivan 12-18). As such, the priestly division of Abijah would have started serving on the second Sabbath of Sivan and worked the following six days. We can surmise that this was the week of Gabriel's visit to Zechariah.

Assuming Zechariah's wife, Elizabeth, conceived John the Baptist soon after Zechariah had finished his Temple service, she would have become pregnant after the third Sabbath of Sivan (approximately Sivan 19-25).

Having a conception date for John allows us to figure out the birthday of Jesus because we know that the angel appeared to Mary to announce that she would bear Jesus when Elizabeth was six months pregnant (Luke 1:23-

33). This would have been Hanukkah, the Jewish Festival of Lights. If we assume that Jesus was conceived about the time of the angel's appearance, that would mean the "Light of the World" (John 1:9, 9:5, 11:9) was conceived during the Festival of Lights. This is just one "coincidental" image in what will become a long list before this chapter is over.

Three months after that, John the Baptist was born, about the time of Passover. This also may be more than coincidence because of the imagery found in the Seder meal. As part of this dinner, Jews place an empty chair at the table for Elijah, hoping that he will soon arrive and fulfill the prophecy of Malachi 4:5 that says that Elijah must return before the Messiah and prepare the way for him. So if our dates are correct, at just the time the Jews were praying for Elijah to return, John the Baptist was born, a man who Jesus said was in fact (at least symbolically) Elijah. Speaking of John, Jesus said, "And if you are willing to accept it, he is the Elijah who was to come" (Matthew 11:14).

Jesus was born six months after Passover, then, in autumn, right around the time of the Festival of Tabernacles.

What Jesus' Birth Date Means to Us

To begin to understand why the actual date of Jesus' birth is important, we need to realize that God often corresponds major historical events to other events in order to help us understand their significance. For instance, we already talked about how Jesus was killed on Passover so that we would better understand that he is the lamb that takes the punishment for sin. We won't go into detail here, but other events that similarly correspond to Jewish holidays would be Jesus' resurrection on the Feast of Firstfruits (Leviticus 23-14, 1 Corinthians 15:20-23), and the outpouring of the Holy

Spirit at the Feast of Weeks (Leviticus 23:15-22, Acts 2), to name but two.

The significance of Jesus being born on the Feast of Tabernacles can be clearly seen when we realize that by descending to earth to take up residence in a human body, Jesus reenacted and fulfilled the act of God descending to earth in the wilderness to take up residence in a tent.

Just as the tabernacles were the temporary dwellings of the sojourning Israelites as they traveled to their permanent home, Canaan, our bodies are our temporary dwellings as we travel across the wilderness of life to our permanent home, Heaven. And just as God came down to help the Israelites along in their quest by living with them in the same type of tent as they were using, Jesus came down to help us along by living with us in the same type of tent that we use: a human body.

That is why John can say, "The Word became flesh and made his dwelling among us. We have seen his glory, the glory of the One and Only, who came from the Father, full of grace and truth" (John 1:14). The term "made his dwelling" in this verse is literally "tabernacled." It comes from the Greek word *skenos*, which means tent or tabernacle and refers to the Hebrew *sukkah*, the singular form of *Sukkot*. John is saying that in Jesus, God took up residence on earth in the same way he did in the desert. By becoming flesh, he set up his tabernacle in the midst of all the rest of the tabernacles so that he might get us through the wilderness. As Matthew explained, this was a fulfillment of a prophecy in Isaiah: "All this took place to fulfill what the Lord had said through the prophet: 'The virgin will be with child and will give birth to a son, and they will call him Immanuel – which means, "God with us"'" (Matthew 1:22-23).

The Holy Spirit

By now you might be thinking, "I see how Jesus could play the same role that God played in the desert, but Jesus is no longer with us. He no longer inhabits an earthly body, so what good will that do us today?" That is a fair question, and it leads us to a discussion of the Holy Spirit.

When Jesus was preparing to leave this world, he comforted his disciples by assuring them that they would not be left alone.

> And I will ask the Father, and he will give you another Counselor to be with you forever – the Spirit of truth. The world cannot accept him, because it neither sees him nor knows him. But you know him, for he lives with you and will be in you. I will not leave you as orphans; I will come to you. Before long, the world will not see me anymore, but you will see me. Because I live, you also will live. On that day you will realize that I am in my Father, and you are in me, and I am in you. (John 14:16-20)

After a brief discussion with Judas, he gave this counselor a name: The Holy Spirit. "All this I have spoken while still with you. But the Counselor, the Holy Spirit, whom the Father will send in my name, will teach you all things and will remind you of everything I have said to you" (John 14:25-26).

Jesus was telling the disciples that they need not worry because when the Holy Spirit comes, God will not just be dwelling in *a* human body, but he will be dwelling in *their* human body. God will actually take up residence inside of them. They will be the tabernacle, or as Paul describes it, God's temple: "Don't you know that you yourselves are God's temple and that God's Spirit lives in you?" (1 Corinthians 3:16).

Jesus described the duties of the Holy Spirit more fully later in the same discourse.

But I tell you the truth: It is for your good that I am going away. Unless I go away, the Counselor will not come to you; but if I go, I will send him to you. When he comes, he will convict the world of guilt in regard to sin and righteousness and judgment: in regard to sin, because men do not believe in me; in regard to righteousness, because I am going to the Father, where you can see me no longer; and in regard to judgment, because the prince of this world now stands condemned.

I have much more to say to you, more than you can now bear. But when he, the Spirit of truth, comes, he will guide you into all truth. He will not speak on his own; he will speak only what he hears, and he will tell you what is yet to come. He will bring glory to me by taking from what is mine and making it known to you. All that belongs to the Father is mine. That is why I said the Spirit will take from what is mine and make it known to you. (John 16:7-15)

Jesus was saying that just as God guided the Israelites during the Exodus and Jesus guided his disciples while on Earth, the Holy Spirit will guide believers after Jesus leaves. Because of this, followers of Jesus today can have hope. Although we have to live in temporary dwellings now, the fact that we have the Holy Spirit living in them with us should be an encouragement. The Holy Spirit provides us with the strength and wisdom to face whatever trials and troubles come our way. This was certainly Paul's argument to the struggling Corinthians. In the midst of a long admonition explaining why they are not to "lose heart" (2 Corinthians 4:1), he said,

> Now we know that if the earthly tent [skenos] we live in is destroyed, we have a building from God, an eternal house in heaven, not built by human hands. Meanwhile we groan, longing to be clothed with our heavenly dwelling, because when we are clothed, we will not be found naked. For while we are in this tent, we groan and are burdened, because we do not wish to be unclothed but to be clothed with our heavenly dwelling, so that what is mortal may be swallowed up by life.

> Now it is God who has made us for this very purpose and has given us the Spirit as a deposit, guaranteeing what is to come. (2 Corinthians 5:1-5)

The Water Libation Ceremony

Another ceremony that was performed during the Feast of Tabernacles (at least during the years that the Temple was in Jerusalem, which would have included Jesus' time) illuminates this truth. It was called the *Nisuch HaMayim*, or "Pouring of the Water." Every morning a priest carrying a golden pitcher led a procession to the pool of Siloam. The priest would fill the pitcher and bring it back through the water gate into Jerusalem and pour it into a receptacle on the altar. After they poured the water, the priests would march around the altar as the people sang the Hallel Psalms (Psalm 113-118) with special emphasis on Psalm 118:25: "O Lord, save us; O Lord, grant us success."

This ceremony was about asking God to bless the upcoming rainy season. It was very joyful, anticipatory and indeed, Messianic. They were thinking of God's miraculous provision of salvific water in the desert as they looked ahead to what God would do to save them in the future, not just from physical drought, but from all oppression. In this spirit, they would refer to Isaiah 12, particularly verse 3 (in italics).

> In that day you will say: "I will praise you, O LORD. Although you were angry with me, your anger has turned away and you have comforted me. Surely God is my salvation; I will trust and not be afraid. The LORD, the LORD, is my strength and my song; he has become my salvation."

> *With joy you will draw water from the wells of salvation.*

> In that day you will say: "Give thanks to the LORD, call on his name; make known among the nations what he has done, and proclaim that his name is exalted. Sing to the LORD, for he has done glorious things; let this be known to all the world. Shout aloud and sing for joy, people of Zion, for great is the Holy One of Israel among you." (Isaiah 12:1-6, emphasis mine)

The Messianic theme was especially strong on the last day of the feast, called *Hashanna Rabba* or the "Great Hosanna." The processional on this morning did not end with just one trip around the altar, but seven. As the priests encircled the sacred place and read Psalm 118, the people waved branches and echoed each line with a loud "Hallelujah." Then, starting in verse 25, they would join in with the phrase, "Hosanna, make your salvation now manifest, Oh Lord." It was a day of extremely joyful Messianic expectation. With this event as a backdrop, Jesus made a very special announcement, which the Apostle John interprets for us:

> On the last and greatest day of the Feast, Jesus stood and said in a loud voice, "If anyone is thirsty, let him come to me and drink. Whoever believes in me, as the Scripture has said, streams of living water will flow from within him." By this he meant the Spirit, whom those who believed in him were later to receive. Up to that time the Spirit had not been given, since Jesus had not yet been glorified. (John 7:37-39)

Just as the people are asking for the Messiah during the biggest day of the Festival of Tabernacles, Jesus stood up and said "Here I am! Are you thirsty for the water that will provide eternal life? I am the source. I will send the Holy Spirit to inhabit you." It is a wonderful image.

In explicitly comparing himself (and the Holy Spirit to follow) to the water provided to the Israelites in the desert, Jesus establishes imagery that was later expounded on by Paul. In talking about the desert wanderers, he explains, "They all ate the same spiritual food and drank the same spiritual drink; for they drank from the spiritual rock that accompanied them, and that rock was Christ" (1 Corinthians 10:3-4).

God will get us across the wilderness by dwelling with us. He comes down and takes up residence in our temporary dwellings in order to guide, protect, and strengthen us as we travel. He enables us to live righteously. Our hope for getting safely home rests in the indwelling (tabernacling) of the Holy Spirit in our bodies.

The Transfiguration
Another event in Jesus' life that may be connected to the Festival of Tabernacles is the transfiguration.

After six days Jesus took Peter, James and John with him and led them up a high mountain, where they were all alone. There he was transfigured before them. His clothes became dazzling white, whiter than anyone in the world could bleach them. And there appeared before them Elijah and Moses, who were talking with Jesus.

Peter said to Jesus, "Rabbi, it is good for us to be here. Let us put up three shelters – one for you, one for Moses and one for Elijah." (He did not know what to say, they were so frightened.)

Then a cloud appeared and enveloped them, and a voice came from the cloud: "This is my Son, whom I love. Listen to him!"

Suddenly, when they looked around, they no longer saw anyone with them except Jesus.

As they were coming down the mountain, Jesus gave them orders not to tell anyone what they had seen until the Son of Man had risen from the dead. They kept the matter to themselves, discussing what "rising from the dead" meant. (Mark 9:2-10)

Jesus had been talking to his disciples about the resurrection and had been trying to convince them that this world is not the end and this body is not their permanent home. At the transfiguration he gave them some evidence for his claims. Not only did he appear to them in a glorified state, but he talked with Moses and Elijah, two dead guys! If life after this body is not possible, what were Moses and Elijah doing there? If their earthly bodies were their permanent home, they would not have been appearing with Jesus.

Peter offers to make some booths for them, which is the reason some scholars think this event took place during the Festival of Tabernacles. Whether it did or not, one of the points being made here is that Moses and Elijah no longer need booths. They no longer live in the temporary home that was their earthly body; they now live in their permanent home. I think they typify two types of people: those who die naturally (Moses, Deuteronomy 34:5) and those who are taken up by God without natural death (Elijah, 2 Kings 2:11). Whether we die naturally or Jesus comes and gets us, we will look back on this body as a temporary shelter for the journey, not our permanent home, and the transfiguration is a good evidence of that.

Peter certainly took this meaning from the event. In trying to encourage his readers to persevere, and fight the good fight, and make it through the wilderness, he said we can take hope in the assurance of our future glorification from the transfiguration. The transfiguration proved that this body is not all there is. Our permanent home awaits.

> So I will always remind you of these things, even though you know them and are firmly established in the truth you now have. I think it is right to refresh your memory as long as I live in the tent [*skenos*] of this body, because I know that I will soon put it aside, as our Lord Jesus Christ has made clear to me. And I will make every effort to

see that after my departure you will always be able to remember these things.

We did not follow cleverly invented stories when we told you about the power and coming of our Lord Jesus Christ, but we were eyewitnesses of his majesty. For he received honor and glory from God the Father when the voice came to him from the Majestic Glory, saying, "This is my Son, whom I love; with him I am well pleased." We ourselves heard this voice that came from heaven when we were with him on the sacred mountain. (2 Peter 1:12-18)

Water of Life for Everyone

Another aspect of the festival that is worth noting is the fact that it is the one festival that is open to everyone. One didn't have to be a Jew to take part. During the "waving of the four species" ceremony, for instance, four types of branches are bound together and waved in all directions (east, west, north, south, up, and down). While there are many levels of meaning to this ceremony, one reason for it is to represent God's mastery of all of creation and his care for all peoples of the world. God is everywhere and for everyone. He invites all to come and partake of the living water. He wants to tabernacle not only with the Jews, but with all people. God wants to send the Holy Spirit to indwell everyone and guide them home.

Zechariah adds some impetus to this invitation by explaining that all nations *must* come to the festival or they will be punished. But notice what the punishment is: they will not receive rain. Understanding that "rain" is symbolic of the Holy Spirit, God is saying that anyone who wants to make it across the wilderness needs the

Holy Spirit and therefore must come, metaphorically, to the Festival of Booths.

> Then the survivors from all the nations that have attacked Jerusalem will go up year after year to worship the King, the LORD Almighty, and to celebrate the Feast of Tabernacles. If any of the peoples of the earth do not go up to Jerusalem to worship the King, the LORD Almighty, they will have no rain. If the Egyptian people do not go up and take part, they will have no rain. The LORD will bring on them the plague he inflicts on the nations that do not go up to celebrate the Feast of Tabernacles. This will be the punishment of Egypt and the punishment of all the nations that do not go up to celebrate the Feast of Tabernacles. (Zechariah 14:16-19)

Those that do not go celebrate God's dwelling with us, who do not appropriate his gracious act, will not be blessed.

Joy to the World
The Festival of Tabernacles was the only festival with the explicit command to be joyful. In Bethlehem, to the singing of angels, God indwelt our tabernacle, our body. He dwelt with us and continues to do so today through the Holy Spirit, so that we might make it to the Promised Land. No matter on which date we celebrate Jesus' birth, that makes it a very merry Christmas.

Chapter 9

The Comfort Trap

Our biblical guidebook, Exodus, ends with the account of God indwelling the tabernacle. The story of the Israelites' journey to the Promised Land is completed in the final three books of Moses (Leviticus, Numbers and Deuteronomy). I want to highlight just two episodes from that part of the story as we conclude this book with two lessons about how to persevere to the end and arrive safely at home.

"Manna for Dinner Again?"

As we pick up the story in Numbers, we find that not even having God dwelling with them in the tabernacle kept the Israelites from grumbling against him.

> Now the people complained about their hardships in the hearing of the LORD, and when he heard them his anger was aroused. Then fire from the LORD burned among them and consumed some of the outskirts of the camp. When the people cried out to Moses, he prayed to the LORD and the fire died down. So that place was called Taberah, because fire from the LORD had burned among them. (Numbers 11:1-3)

Traveling across the wilderness was difficult. Living as nomads in the scorching desert with enemies all around isn't anybody's idea of a comfortable or pleasant existence. The Israelites didn't like it and they let God know. Unfortunately for them, God didn't see the value in their complaining and judgment fell. However, even that didn't stop the grumbling. "The rabble with them began to crave other food, and again the Israelites started wailing and said, 'If only we had meat to eat! We remember the fish we ate in Egypt at no cost – also the cucumbers, melons, leeks, onions and garlic. But now we have lost our appetite; we never see anything but this manna!'" (Numbers 11:4-6). This didn't sit well with God, either. He gave Moses these instructions:

> "Tell the people: 'Consecrate yourselves in preparation for tomorrow, when you will eat meat. The Lord heard you when you wailed, "If only we had meat to eat! We were better off in Egypt!" Now the LORD will give you meat, and you will eat it. You will not eat it for just one day, or two days, or five, ten or twenty days, but for a whole month – until it comes out of your nostrils and you loathe it – because you have rejected the LORD, who is among you, and have wailed before him, saying, "Why did we ever leave Egypt?"'" (Numbers 11:18-20)

Be careful what you wish for, the old saying goes, you just might get it.

> Now a wind went out from the LORD and drove quail in from the sea. It brought them down all around the camp to about three feet above the ground, as far as a day's walk in any direction. All that day and night and all the next day the people went out and gathered quail. No one gathered less than ten homers. Then they spread them out all around the camp. But while the meat was still between their teeth and before it could be consumed, the anger of the Lord burned against

the people, and he struck them with a severe plague. Therefore the place was named Kibroth Hattaavah, because there they buried the people who had craved other food. (Numbers 11:31-34)

So we have two more incidents in which God became angry and judged the people because of their grumbling. The Israelites complained first about general hardships and then about not having enough variety in their menu. They had griped about food before, of course, but notice the difference this time. When the Israelites complained previously about not having water to drink or bread to eat, they were concerned for their very survival – they were worried about dying in the desert. That was not a factor in this case, as there was plenty of food and water to keep the people nourished. This time they were after variety. The Israelites were tired of manna and wanted some meat. They were past looking for simply survival. They no longer wanted to just get by; they wanted prosperity.

Evaluating these two events together, we can summarize by saying that the Israelites were complaining because they wanted a higher degree of comfort than they were experiencing. They wanted a life with more ease and fancier food. They wanted more, to borrow a term from Francis Schaeffer, "personal peace and affluence."

> Personal peace means just to be let alone, not to be troubled by the troubles of other people, whether across the world or across the city – to live one's life with minimal possibilities of being personally disturbed. Personal peace means wanting to have my personal life pattern undisturbed in my lifetime, regardless of what the result will be in the lifetimes of my children and grandchildren.

Affluence means an overwhelming and ever-increasing prosperity – a life made up of things, things, and more things – a success judged by an ever-higher level of material advance.[23]

Schaeffer aptly describes the longings of the Israelites. We see their desire for personal peace in their grumbling about "hardships." They no longer wanted to be disturbed by enemies, heat, sandstorms and all the other things that made the journey difficult. We see their desire for affluence in the request for meat. They were not content with the necessities of life; they wanted some luxuries.

The Problem with Choosing Personal Peace and Prosperity

So what is the problem? What is so wrong with a little peace and prosperity? Why did God get so angry with the Israelites?

The key to the answer is found in remembering their situation. The Israelites were in the midst of a journey and a battle. They were on a trip to the Promised Land that involved fighting against harsh conditions and human enemies. They were sojourners and they were soldiers. Put another way, I think we could accurately label them athletes and warriors. They were striving to complete a race and win a fight. As such, the last thing the people should have been expecting is comfort. The reason for this, of course, is that to be a successful athlete or soldier, one has to sacrifice personal peace and prosperity. Athletes and soldiers have to give up comfort in order to gain victory.

For instance, think of what it takes to win the Tour de France. Riding a bicycle for hundreds of miles over multiple mountain passes is anything but comfortable. Muscles ache, lungs burn, and I am quite sure every part of the cyclist's body longs for it to be over. However, a champion must keep going through the pain. The only alternative is to lose. If, in the middle of the race, the rider chooses peace for his sore muscles by stopping, he doesn't win. It's as simple as that. Or think of what it takes to win a war. What could be less comfortable and peaceful for a soldier than a firefight? Yet victory requires that these battles be fought. To choose comfort in a war is to lose the war. Refusing to fight because the pain of battle is too great is simply to surrender. Personal peace must be sacrificed to win races and fights. Embracing hardship is essential to victory. The Israelites made the mistake of not doing that.

In regard to prosperity, the same principle holds true. Consider again what athletes and soldiers go through to gain success. While others are sleeping in, they are at the gym shooting baskets, in the pool swimming laps, or at the rifle range taking shots. While others are lounging in front of the television with a bowl of popcorn, they are in the weight room working out. While others are lazing at the beach, they are at summer training camp. Soldiers and athletes give up certain levels of prosperity in order to achieve a level of excellence that will lead them to victory. They deny themselves some extravagances and accept a more modest lifestyle because this type of discipline is necessary to win. Prosperity must be sacrificed for victory. The Israelites failed to do this as well. They fell into what I refer to as the comfort trap.

The Four Soils

The desire for personal peace and prosperity is one of the great obstacles to victory in the Christian life. The comfort trap keeps many people out of the Promised Land, as Jesus made plain in the parable of the soils:

That same day Jesus went out of the house and sat by the lake. Such large crowds gathered around him that he got into a boat and sat in it, while all the people stood on the shore. Then he told them many things in parables, saying: "A farmer went out to sow his seed. As he was scattering the seed, some fell along the path, and the birds came and ate it up. Some fell on rocky places, where it did not have much soil. It sprang up quickly, because the soil was shallow. But when the sun came up, the plants were scorched, and they withered because they had no root. Other seed fell among thorns, which grew up and choked the plants. Still other seed fell on good soil, where it produced a crop—a hundred, sixty or thirty times what was sown. He who has ears, let him hear." (Matthew 13:1-9)

Jesus went on to explain the parable.

Listen then to what the parable of the sower means: When anyone hears the message about the kingdom and does not understand it, the evil one comes and snatches away what was sown in his heart. This is the seed sown along the path. The one who received the seed that fell on rocky places is the man who hears the word and at once receives it with joy. But since he has no root, he lasts only a short time. When trouble or persecution comes because of the word, he quickly falls away. The one who received the seed that fell among the thorns is the man who hears the word, but the worries of this life and the deceitfulness of wealth choke it, making it unfruitful. But the one who received the seed that fell on good soil is the man who hears the word and understands it. He produces a crop, yielding a hundred, sixty or thirty times what was sown. (Matthew 13:18-23)

The four types of soil are four types of people. All four hear the message of the Kingdom, and three start producing a crop. In other words, three start traveling across the wilderness, walking the narrow road. However, two of those three fail to finish the journey. Two of the three ultimately fail to produce fruit. What causes them to fail? According to Jesus, it is persecution (verse 21), the worries of this life, and the deceitfulness of wealth (verse 22). These people are brought down because they run into hardships in the form of persecution and day-to-day worries and they chase after material wealth, which can never satisfy. Notice what kept these people from the Kingdom. The soils that didn't produce fruit are those that chose *personal peace and prosperity* over Jesus. They chose comfort over truth, ease of life over victory. They were not good athletes or soldiers.

Peter exhibited these characteristics when Jesus was on trial. Even after vowing to stay with Jesus through thick and thin (Mark 14:29), Peter denied he even knew Jesus when the going got too tough (Mark 14:66-72). Peter was brought down by a desire for comfort in the midst of persecution. Of course, Peter later became one of the most courageous evangelists in the world and was ultimately martyred for his savior, but in the episode at Jesus' trial, he failed.

It is not easy to live as an athlete or soldier. It is not easy to live in discomfort. However, it can be done. Indeed, it must be done, but how?

Two Measures

There are two important measures we can take that are indispensable for persevering through discomfort and defeating the desire for personal peace and prosperity. First we need to remember that this world is not our home. Second, we need to keep focused on the goal: our true home, Heaven. Although these actions are basically two sides of the same coin, I think it is helpful to speak of them separately.

This World Is Not Our Home

First, remember that this world is not our home. Don't expect it to feel like home.

I have had the pleasure of speaking at a Bible Camp in northern Canada a couple of times. The camp is located in a beautiful spot, but frankly it is not a very comfortable place to stay. The cabins are old, the mosquitoes are massive, and the ground is covered in fine sand that gets everywhere. Everyone walks around in varying states of grubbiness all week. However, I had a wonderful time there; it never crossed my mind to complain about the conditions. In fact, I hardly ever heard a camper complain about them either.

The reason for this lack of concern about the conditions is, of course, that we were *camping*! Camping is not supposed to be comfortable. It is not supposed to have all the amenities of home. The whole idea is to get away from home and rough it for a while. Neither the campers nor I complained because we weren't expecting anything better. Those that complained didn't understand camping. The rest of us realized that the camp was not our home and that we would leave it in a short time. We were at the camp not to settle down, but to accomplish certain tasks and then leave. I was there to speak; they were there to make friends, learn and have fun. After that mission was accomplished, we would all go get comfortable again. With that mindset, putting up with a little discomfort was not difficult at all.

On the other hand, if I had gone to the camp expecting to have all the amenities of home or had gone there with a different objective than I did, I probably would have been miserable and ineffective. However, the fault would have been mine for having improper expectations and for not realizing my true situation.

This is why God was so angry with the Israelites. They should have remembered their situation and their mission and adjusted their mindset accordingly. They were sojourners in the wilderness, traveling campers as it were. That they expected all the comforts of the Promised Land (or Egypt) was not reasonable and showed they had strayed from their mission and forgotten what they were doing. Athletes in the middle of a race and soldiers in the middle of a fight should not expect to feel as comfortable as they do when they are home resting on the sofa. If they start to believe that races and battles should be comfortable, they will certainly lose.

Keeping our Eyes on the Prize

The second principle goes with the first. Not only do we need to remember that this is not our home, but we also need to focus on the place that is our home. We need to keep remembering the goal of our journey, Heaven. We must keep our eyes on the prize.

Top athletes are driven by one thing: being the best. They are focused on the prize that comes with victory. To win the Tour de France, for example, one must have a single-minded obsession with winning and getting to wear that yellow champion's jersey. Only those who can keep that at the forefront of their thoughts, rather than the pain of the cramping in their thigh, will have a chance.

During their run to the National Hockey League finals in 2003, the coach of the Anaheim Mighty Ducks brought the Stanley Cup into the team's dressing room so that his players could focus on it and envision themselves carrying it around the ice in victory. He wanted them to be clear about what they were sacrificing all their time and effort for. He understood that those who cannot see the goal cannot accomplish it. Of course, keeping your eyes on the prize does not guarantee victory – the Ducks eventually lost – but it certainly makes winning much more likely. Clearly seeing the objective of the struggle is essential.

In the same way, soldiers need to be able to focus on the purpose for which they are fighting. If they can envision the gains a victory will bring, sacrifice will come easier. Soldiers that can focus on the big prize will be able to face the struggle with the strength to make it through the pain. As soon as soldiers lose sight of that prize (or do not believe there is a reward worth fighting for), all is lost.

Applying this principle to the Exodus story, the Israelites should have kept thinking about Canaan, the land flowing with milk and honey. If they had kept the country of promise at the forefront of their thoughts, they wouldn't have been so bogged down by the troubles that came their way. They needed to be driven, just as any athlete or soldier, by their desire to gain that prize.

For us, this means being driven by the reward of Heaven. We need to have a single-minded obsession with getting to our true home and enjoying that prize. The great men and women of faith certainly did. In fact, the primary characteristic of the heroes listed in Hebrews 11 is their obsession with Heaven. As we survey these saints, notice what motivated them: they realized that this world was not their home and they stayed focused on the prize they would receive at the end of their journey.

What Drove the Heroes of Faith

After praising the faith of Abel and Enoch, the author of Hebrews explains that "without faith it is impossible to please God, because anyone who comes to him must believe that he exists and that he rewards those who earnestly seek him" (Hebrews 11:6). Trusting that God will reward his servants is an essential part of faith. Obedience flows from being sure that it will be worth it in the end. We trust that the reward will be great and focus on it as an encouragement to persevere. Look at the Abraham's story, for example:

> By faith Abraham, when called to go to a place he would later receive as his inheritance, obeyed and went, even though he did not know where he was going. By faith he made his home in the Promised Land like a stranger in a foreign country; he lived in tents, as did Isaac and Jacob, who were heirs with him of the same promise. For he was looking forward to the city with foundations, whose architect and builder is God. (Hebrews 11:8-10)

Abraham lived in tents as a sojourner, just like his descendents later would. And just like they should have but didn't, he accepted his predicament without complaining. There are two reasons he was able to do this: Abraham realized that he wasn't home yet and was focused on the future. He understood that one day he would lay aside his tent for the solid structures of Heaven and he continually looked forward to this reward.

After explaining what motivated Abraham, the author of Hebrews then summarizes the first part of the chapter by explaining that all the rest of the faith heroes were driven by their longing for Heaven as well.

> All these people were still living by faith when they died. They did not receive the things promised; they only saw them and welcomed them from a distance. And they admitted that they were aliens and strangers on earth. People who say such things show that they are looking for a country of their own. If they had been thinking of the country they had left, they would have had opportunity to return. Instead, they were longing for a better country – a heavenly one. Therefore God is not ashamed to be called their God, for he has prepared a city for them. (Hebrews 11:13-16)

Here is a perfect example of taking the two measures I have recommended. The people remembered that this world is not their home ("admitted that they were aliens and strangers on earth") and they kept their eyes on Heaven ("they were longing for a better country – a heavenly one"). God was proud to prepare a place for them.

Later in the passage we learn what motivated Moses to give up royalty and identify with his people. He had his eyes on the prize.

> By faith Moses, when he had grown up, refused to be known as the son of Pharaoh's daughter. He chose to be mistreated along with the people of God rather than to enjoy the pleasures of sin for a short time. He regarded disgrace for the sake of Christ as of greater value than the treasures of

Egypt, because he was looking ahead to his reward. (Hebrews 11:24-26)

Moses chose to give up the personal peace and prosperity of his life in Pharaoh's palace so that he could gain a much bigger reward. His example was followed by many, many others. In fact, a few verses later we read about men and women who not only met with discomfort, but willingly gave up their lives so that they would gain "a better resurrection." People don't get more Heaven-focused than this:

> Others were tortured and refused to be released, so that they might gain a better resurrection. Some faced jeers and flogging, while still others were chained and put in prison. They were stoned; they were sawed in two; they were put to death by the sword. They went about in sheepskins and goatskins, destitute, persecuted and mistreated – the world was not worthy of them. They wandered in deserts and mountains, and in caves and holes in the ground.

> These were all commended for their faith, yet none of them received what had been promised. God had planned something better for us so that only together with us would they be made perfect. (Hebrews 11:35b-40)

"The world was not worthy of them!" What a wonderful way to be remembered. These giants of faith did not receive their reward while on earth, but they weren't expecting it on earth. The reward they had been promised was Heaven.

The practical application for us is clear: "Therefore, since we are surrounded by such a great cloud of witnesses, let us throw off everything that hinders and the sin that so easily entangles, and let us run with perseverance the race marked out for us" (Hebrews 12:1). We are to be like these spiritual masters. We are not to get bogged down by persecutions, the worries of this life and the deceitfulness of wealth. We are not to let the desire for personal peace and prosperity keep us from running the race to the end. We are to keep our eyes firmly on the prize.

To finish the argument, the author of Hebrews then gives us the ultimate example to follow. In the matter of focusing on future rewards to get us through tough times, we are, in fact, to be like Jesus. "Let us fix our eyes on Jesus, the author and perfecter of our faith, who for the joy set before him endured the cross, scorning its shame, and sat down at the right hand of the throne of God. Consider him who endured such opposition from sinful men, so that you will not grow weary and lose heart" (Hebrews 12:2-3).

What enabled Jesus to persevere when he was at his lowest point? The joy set before him! Jesus had a clear vision of the reward he would receive at the end of his service. He saw himself sitting down at the right hand of the throne of God. According to this passage, Jesus was able to withstand the beatings and the cross because he had his mind focused on Heaven. He had his eyes on the prize. We are to do the same. Setting our eyes on the prize will keep us from growing weary and losing heart in the middle of the wilderness.

Paul so longed to win the prize of Heaven that the thought of sharing in Christ's sufferings to get it was actually appealing to him.

> I want to know Christ and the power of his resurrection and the fellowship of sharing in his sufferings, becoming like him in his death, and so,

somehow, to attain to the resurrection from the dead.

Not that I have already obtained all this, or have already been made perfect, but I press on to take hold of that for which Christ Jesus took hold of me. Brothers, I do not consider myself yet to have taken hold of it. But one thing I do: Forgetting what is behind and straining toward what is ahead, I press on toward the goal to win the prize for which God has called me heavenward in Christ Jesus. (Philippians 3:10-14)

Paul didn't spend his life running the race and fighting the fight in order to lose. Paul wanted that reward, and he focused accordingly:

Do you not know that in a race all the runners run, but only one gets the prize? Run in such a way as to get the prize. Everyone who competes in the games goes into strict training. They do it to get a crown that will not last; but we do it to get a crown that will last forever. Therefore I do not run like a man running aimlessly; I do not fight like a man beating the air. No, I beat my body and make it my slave so that after I have preached to others, I myself will not be disqualified for the prize. (1 Corinthians 9:24-27)

Paul succeeded in his quest. These are some of his last recorded words:

For I am already being poured out like a drink offering, and the time has come for my departure. I have fought the good fight, I have finished the race, I have kept the faith. Now there is in store

for me the crown of righteousness, which the
Lord, the righteous Judge, will award to me on
that day – and not only to me, but also to all who
have longed for his appearing. (2 Timothy 4:6-8)

Paul longed for the day of Christ's appearing because
he knew that would be the day when he would finally
get his prize. The race would be over, the battle won. He
took this promise of Jesus seriously: "Behold, I am
coming soon! My reward is with me, and I will give to
everyone according to what he has done" (Revelation
22:12-13). We need to meditate on that promise at all times.
Whenever our vision of that great day becomes blurry,
we are in danger of falling into the comfort trap.

Addressing a Possible Objection
Before we leave this chapter, let me quickly address
one possible objection. Some people have told me that it
seems like I am advocating a mindset that views the
reward at the end of our journey as rightful payment for
all the suffering we have gone through on the way to
getting it. This is not what I am saying at all. The reward
of the Promised Land is God's gift. We don't earn it.
However, that does not mean that we are not to focus on
the fact that we will receive that gift, if we make it
through the wilderness, as motivation to persevere. If I
tell my daughter she will get to open a special present as
soon as she has finished her chores for the day, it does
not mean that the present is payment for the chores.
However, she can still focus on the present as
encouragement and motivation to persevere through her
duties. The fact that we have the chance to go to Heaven
is an overwhelming act of God's grace. However, that
does not make it any less valuable to receive and

therefore does not make it any less powerful as a motivating tool.

Chapter 10

The Trustworthiness of God

When Looking Ahead is not Enough

Defeating the desire for personal peace and affluence is not the only thing we need to do to stay on the narrow way. Satan has many more cards to play than that, and we need to counter with a multifaceted battle plan of our own.

One of the devil's most effective attacks involves tempting us to despair by telling us that the path we are on is leading to catastrophe. Naturally, he uses this lie at those times when the future looks bleak: when roadblocks seem insurmountable and the struggle too hard. These are critical moments in life as they force us to decide, "Are we going to live in faith and do what we know God wants us to do, even in the face of much apparent trouble and danger – or not?" Satan comes and whispers in our ear one of his most powerful lies: "God is not trustworthy. Don't do it."

Satan's strategy is to try to bring into doubt God's character or his power. (Satan may also attempt to get you to question other things like God's existence, but this seems to occur less often and be less effective. People don't usually doubt God's existence; they are just not sure about following him.) The deceiver says, "God will let you fall. He will let the water crash in around you. He will let you be defeated by your enemies. He doesn't have your best interests at heart, and even if he does, he doesn't have the ability to make his desires happen. Following him will be disastrous. Don't obey. Don't follow."

Against these lies, it does not help to follow the advice of last chapter and keep our eyes on the prize (although we should keep doing that to combat Satan's other lies), because the reward will not entice us if we are not sure that God is willing and able to come through with it. In combating the devil's attacks on God's trustworthiness, meditating on God's promises is of little use. However, there is something we can do. We can focus on God's faithfulness in the past. As we examine the existing evidence of God's power and goodness, Satan's attempt at sabotaging our journey will be seen for the ruse that it is.

If only more of the Israelites had followed this principle. Their experience at the very edge of the Promised Land provides another stellar example of what not to do.

Doubt at Kadesh Barnea
The journey of the Israelites finally seemed to be near an end. They had reached the border of Canaan and camped at a place called Kadesh Barnea. At God's request, Moses chose 12 men to spy out the land in preparation for conquest.

They gave Moses this account: "We went into the land to which you sent us, and it does flow with milk and honey! Here is its fruit. But the people who live there are powerful, and the cities are fortified and very large. We even saw descendants of Anak there. The Amalekites live in the Negev; the Hittites, Jebusites and Amorites live in the hill country; and the Canaanites live near the sea and along the Jordan."

Then Caleb silenced the people before Moses and said, "We should go up and take possession of the land, for we can certainly do it."

But the men who had gone up with him said, "We can't attack those people; they are stronger than we are." And they spread among the Israelites a bad report about the land they had explored. They said, "The land we explored devours those living in it. All the people we saw there are of great size. We saw the Nephilim there (the descendants of Anak come from the Nephilim). We seemed like grasshoppers in our own eyes, and we looked the same to them."

That night all the people of the community raised their voices and wept aloud. All the Israelites grumbled against Moses and Aaron, and the whole assembly said to them, "If only we had died in Egypt! Or in this desert! Why is the LORD bringing us to this land only to let us fall by the sword? Our wives and children will be taken as plunder. Wouldn't it be better for us to go back to Egypt?" And they said to each other, "We should choose a leader and go back to Egypt."

Then Moses and Aaron fell facedown in front of the whole Israelite assembly gathered there. Joshua son of Nun and Caleb son of Jephunneh, who were among those who had explored the land, tore their clothes and said to the entire Israelite assembly, "The land we passed through and explored is exceedingly good. If the Lord is pleased with us, he will lead us into that land, a land flowing with milk and honey, and will give it to us. Only do not rebel against the Lord. And do not be afraid of the people of the land, because we will swallow them up. Their protection is gone, but the Lord is with us. Do not be afraid of them."

But the whole assembly talked about stoning them. (Numbers 13:27-14:10a)

The Israelites were at a critical point of decision. God had told them to take the land, but they were afraid of its current inhabitants. The obstacles to victory looked too big. In other words, they simply didn't think God had the ability or willingness to do what he had promised and conquer their enemies and therefore they didn't want to obey. They didn't think God could be trusted. Of the spies, only Caleb and Joshua believed God could do it. These men, along with Moses and Aaron, were eager to take the land, but they could not convince the rest of the people.

As a result, God sent the Hebrews back out into the wilderness to wander for forty years. None of the people (20 years old or older) who grumbled against God got to enter the land. They all died in the desert (Numbers 14:26-35).

The Israelites believed Satan's lie. They succumbed to irrational fear. I say their fear was irrational because the people were not being asked to take a blind leap of faith at Kadesh Barnea. God wasn't new to them. They hadn't just met him. The people should have known that God was trustworthy. They had seen his power and goodness over and over again. He had always been faithful to take care of them in any and every situation. All they needed to do was remember this, and they would have been fine. They had plenty of good reasons to trust in him.

This is what made God so angry. He had given them abundant evidence of his trustworthiness, yet they still wouldn't step out in faith and obey.

Then the glory of the LORD appeared at the Tent of Meeting to all the Israelites. The LORD said to

Moses, "How long will these people treat me with contempt? How long will they refuse to believe in me, in spite of all the miraculous signs I have performed among them? I will strike them down with a plague and destroy them, but I will make you into a nation greater and stronger than they." (Numbers 14:10b-12)

In spite of all the miraculous signs, in spite of all the evidence of God's power and goodness, the Israelites refused to trust.

The Power of Praise

There is a simple antidote to fear of the future and lack of faith in God: praising him for what he has done in the past. Instead of grumbling and cowering at the report of giant cities and powerful men, the Israelites should have had a time of prayer and praise, thanking God for his wonderful work in getting them to this point. After spending some time remembering the plagues and the Red Sea and the provision of manna from Heaven and water from the rock and the victory over the Amalekites, etc., they almost certainly would have been willing to enter the land expecting to see God perform more miracles.

The act of recounting the stories and thanking God for what he has done puts a person in the frame of mind necessary to obediently step out in faith. It shines the light of truth on the present situation and destroys the lie that God is not trustworthy.

This is exactly what in an episode in the reign of King Jehoshaphat. Judah looked as if it was going to be overrun by a powerful army. Rather than despair, however, the king called the people together for prayer and praise.

Then Jehoshaphat stood up in the assembly of Judah and Jerusalem at the temple of the LORD in the front of the new courtyard and said:

"O LORD, God of our fathers, are you not the God who is in heaven? You rule over all the kingdoms of the nations. Power and might are in your hand, and no one can withstand you. O our God, did you not drive out the inhabitants of this land before your people Israel and give it forever to the descendants of Abraham your friend? They have lived in it and have built in it a sanctuary for your Name, saying, 'If calamity comes upon us, whether the sword of judgment, or plague or famine, we will stand in your presence before this temple that bears your Name and will cry out to you in our distress, and you will hear us and save us.'

"But now here are men from Ammon, Moab and Mount Seir, whose territory you would not allow Israel to invade when they came from Egypt; so they turned away from them and did not destroy them. See how they are repaying us by coming to drive us out of the possession you gave us as an inheritance. O our God, will you not judge them? For we have no power to face this vast army that is attacking us. We do not know what to do, but our eyes are upon you." (2 Chronicles 20:5-12)

Notice the confidence inspiring content of the prayer. Jehoshaphat started by ascribing to God all power and then backed up this claim by recounting what God had done in the past in giving Israel the land. With his mind focused on God's faithfulness in the past, Jehoshaphat could look confidently towards the future, knowing that

God is trustworthy and will keep his promises. When asked to step out in faith and face the army, Jehoshaphat obeyed, even though it looked like a fool's errand, and God provided a great victory (2 Chronicles 20:14-29). God would have done the same for the Israelites at Kadesh Barnea, but they refused to remember all that he had done and were therefore unwilling to obey in faith. They focused on the strength of the enemy rather than the strength of God. In later years their ancestors would make the same mistake in the valley of Elah. Thankfully, there was one among them who had experienced and remembered God's power and goodness.

David and Goliath

It is one of the most famous tales in the history of the world, but let's take a moment to reacquaint ourselves with the story of David and Goliath.

Israel was at war with the Philistines and the two armies had drawn up battle lines on either side of the Valley of Elah, with the Philistines employing an interesting strategy.

A champion named Goliath, who was from Gath, came out of the Philistine camp. He was over nine feet tall. He had a bronze helmet on his head and wore a coat of scale armor of bronze weighing five thousand shekels; on his legs he wore bronze greaves, and a bronze javelin was slung on his back. His spear shaft was like a weaver's rod, and its iron point weighed six hundred shekels. His shield bearer went ahead of him.

Goliath stood and shouted to the ranks of Israel, "Why do you come out and line up for battle? Am I not a Philistine, and are you not the servants of

Saul? Choose a man and have him come down to me. If he is able to fight and kill me, we will become your subjects; but if I overcome him and kill him, you will become our subjects and serve us." Then the Philistine said, "This day I defy the ranks of Israel! Give me a man and let us fight each other." On hearing the Philistine's words, Saul and all the Israelites were dismayed and terrified. (1 Samuel 17:4-11)

This taunting continued for over a month until one day the shepherd boy David arrived to check on his brothers and see how the battle was going (1 Samuel 17:16-20). While David was talking with the troops, Goliath made his daily appearance within earshot of the youngster (1 Samuel 17:23). David asked around about what would be done for the man who killed Goliath and word of his inquiries got back to King Saul, who summoned David (1 Samuel 17:25-31).

In the discussion that followed, notice what gave David the confidence to face Goliath. David was not afraid of the mighty soldier because he was aware of what God had done for David in the past.

> David said to Saul, "Let no one lose heart on account of this Philistine; your servant will go and fight him."

> Saul replied, "You are not able to go out against this Philistine and fight him; you are only a boy, and he has been a fighting man from his youth."

> But David said to Saul, "Your servant has been keeping his father's sheep. When a lion or a bear came and carried off a sheep from the flock, I went after it, struck it and rescued the sheep from

its mouth. When it turned on me, I seized it by its hair, struck it and killed it. Your servant has killed both the lion and the bear; this uncircumcised Philistine will be like one of them, because he has defied the armies of the living God. The LORD who delivered me from the paw of the lion and the paw of the bear will deliver me from the hand of this Philistine."

Saul said to David, "Go, and the LORD be with you." (1 Samuel 17:32-37)

David knew that God was able to help him defeat Goliath because God had helped him defeat strong enemies before. While everyone else looked at Goliath and saw only certain defeat, David remembered what God had done to the bear and the lion and saw sure victory. By keeping his mind on God's past mighty works, David was able to affirm God's trustworthiness and take a huge step of faith with confidence.

David was in the very same position as the Israelites at Kadesh Barnea. Both were faced with the option of either following God and stepping into battle with a very strong foe or turning around and running in fear. David looked back, realized God was trustworthy, and took a step of faith. The Israelites didn't. They looked only at the obstacle in front of them, never looking back at what God had done, and ended up dying in the desert for lack of faith.

May we follow the example of David and not the Israelites. The longer we walk with Jesus and experience his power and goodness, the stronger our faith should be. When faced with one of those situations that seems sure to end in catastrophe, we should be able to look back at all God has done and face the future with confidence, knowing he can handle it.

Jesus Calms the Storm

Jesus' disciples were a little slow in learning this lesson, as demonstrated in the following episode.

That day when evening came, he said to his disciples, "Let us go over to the other side." Leaving the crowd behind, they took him along, just as he was, in the boat. There were also other boats with him. A furious squall came up, and the waves broke over the boat, so that it was nearly swamped. Jesus was in the stern, sleeping on a cushion. The disciples woke him and said to him, "Teacher, don't you care if we drown?"

He got up, rebuked the wind and said to the waves, "Quiet! Be still!" Then the wind died down and it was completely calm.

He said to his disciples, "Why are you so afraid? Do you still have no faith?" (Mark 4:35-40)

The important word in that last sentence is "still." The key to understanding Jesus' rebuke is to realize that the disciples had already seen Jesus do many miraculous signs and wonders. He had shown his power and goodness in casting out demons and healing many sick and lame (Mark 1:21-3:12). The proper response to the storm would have been to remember that Jesus had been willing and able to exert authority over every other realm of existence (see Chapter 2), and surmise that he could handle this, too. The disciples obviously did not do this, as they were convinced that death was immanent.

Remembering God's faithfulness is a very difficult thing to do, especially when the wind is blowing hard and it seems like the waves will swamp us, but we must do it if we are ever going to stride boldly into the Promised Land.

Finally Home

Striding boldly into the Promised Land is exactly what Joshua did 40 years after the debacle at Kadesh Barnea. One of the two spies who trusted God, Joshua had the privilege of finally leading the Israelites into Canaan. As we conclude this chapter and this book, let me encourage you with the words that God gave to Joshua as he prepared to cross the Jordon River into Canaan.

> Your territory will extend from the desert to Lebanon, and from the great river, the Euphrates – all the Hittite country – to the Great Sea on the west. No one will be able to stand up against you all the days of your life. As I was with Moses, so I will be with you; I will never leave you nor forsake you.

> Be strong and courageous, because you will lead these people to inherit the land I swore to their forefathers to give them. Be strong and very courageous. Be careful to obey all the law my servant Moses gave you; do not turn from it to the right or to the left, that you may be successful wherever you go. Do not let this Book of the Law depart from your mouth; meditate on it day and night, so that you may be careful to do everything written in it. Then you will be prosperous and successful. Have I not commanded you? Be strong and courageous. Do not be terrified; do not be discouraged, for the LORD your God will be with you wherever you go. (Joshua 1:4-9)

The narrow road across the wilderness to Heaven is long and difficult and full of traps, but you can travel it successfully because God will be with you. Be strong and courageous. Fight the good fight. Finish the race. I'll see you at home.

Notes

1. Gregg Easterbrook notes that while essentially everything about today's life is materially better than our ancestors, we are not happy:

> …how many of us feel positive about our moment, or even believe that life is getting better? Today Americans tell pollsters that the country is going downhill; that their parents had it better; that they feel unbearably stressed out; that their children face a declining future. …
>
> The percentage of Americans who describe themselves as "happy" has not budged since the 1950s, though the typical person's real income has more than doubled through that period. Happiness has not increased in Japan or Western Europe in the past half-century, either, though daily life in both those places has grown fantastically better, incorporating all the advances noted above plus the end of dictatorships and recovery from war… [Even in an era of abundance and social progress] the citizens of the United States and the European Union, almost all of whom live better than almost all of the men and women in history, entertain considerable discontent. (Gregg Easterbrook, *The Progress Paradox: How Life Gets Better While People Feel Worse* (New York: Random House, 2004), xv-xvi.)

2. I will not take time here to present the full "argument from desire." I encourage everyone to read *Mere Christianity* by C.S. Lewis for proper treatment of this subject.

3. C.S. Lewis, *Mere Christianity* (New York: Collier Books, 1960), 120.

4. When I use the term "Heaven" in this book, I am using it in a general sense to refer to that state of existence in which those that are saved will live for eternity. I am not making dogmatic assertions about the specific nature of that existence other than to say it will be perfect because we will be with God. For the purposes of this book,

I am defining Heaven as simply the "life" spoken of in Matthew 7:14.

5. Randy Alcorn, *Heaven* (Wheaton: Tyndale, 2004), 160.

6. This book is not a traditional commentary on Exodus. I do not exegete every passage in the book, nor do I explore the depths of meaning of every verse that I do interpret. Also, I do not walk through the story chronologically, although most of the major episodes will get covered at some point.

7. Jean Danielou, *The Bible and the Liturgy* (Notre Dame, IN: University of Notre Dame Press, 1956), 75

8.http://biologos.org/blog/yahweh-creation-and-the-cosmic-battle/

9. Optatus of Milan, *Donat.* V, 1; PL, 11, 1041 quoted in Jean Danielou, "The Sacraments and the History of Salvation" http://www.catholicculture.org/culture/library/view.cfm?recnum=6 81

10. For a nicely balanced short article on the three tenses of salvation, see "Salvation: Past, Present of Future?" in Walter C. Kaiser Jr., Peter H. Davids, F.F. Bruce, and Manfred T. Brauch, *The Hard Sayings of The Bible* (Downers Grove: InterVarsity Press, 1996), 709-710. According to the Bible, Christians have been saved, are being saved and will be saved, with the emphasis on the future tense.

11. Jean Danielou, *God and the Ways of Knowing* (San Francisco: Ignatius Press, 2003), 122

12. Dietrich Bonhoeffer, *The Cost of Discipleship* (New York: Touchstone, 1995), 89.

13. http://www.wheaton.edu/bgc/archives/faq/20.htm

14. I owe the phrases "God's passion for his glory," as well as much of this argument, to John Piper, *God's Passion for His Glory* (Wheaton: Crossway, 1998).

15. Jonathan Edwards, *The Religious Affections*, John Smith, ed., *The Works of Jonathan Edwards*, vol. 2 (New Haven: Yale University Press, 1959), 249-50.

16. Piper, 34-35.

17. For a fuller discussion of the poll data, see Ronald J. Sider, *The Scandal of the Evangelical Conscience* (Grand Rapids, Baker, 2005).

18. www.blazinggrace.org/pornstatistics.htm.

19. Sider, 17.

20. Arthur W. Pink, *Studies on Saving Faith* (Swengel, PA, Reiner Publications, publication date unknown. The Publisher's "Preface" states: "To give the reader a clearer appreciation of this book, it should be stated that the materials found herein were first published in 1932, 1933, and 1937, in *Studies in the Scriptures*, a monthly magazine published by Mr. Pink from 1922 to 1953.") The full text of this book is readily available for free on the internet. This particular quotation can be found at www.pbministries.org/books/pink/Saving_Faith/saving_faith_part1.htm.

21. Charles H Spurgeon, *Morning and Evening*, February 8 Evening. This book is also public domain and readily available for free on the internet. One place to find it is www.ccel.org/ccel/spurgeon/morneve.html.

22. Christine A. Scheller, "A Divine Conspirator," *Christianity Today* vol. 50, no. 9 (2006), 45.

23. Francis A. Schaffer, *How Should We Then Live* (Wheaton: Crossway, 1976), 205.

Made in the USA
Lexington, KY
23 July 2012